Frugal Isn't Cheap

Frugal Isn't Cheap

Spend Less, Save More, and Live BETTER

Clare K. Levison, CPA

The Career Press, Inc.
Pompton Plains, NJ

FRUGAL ISN'T CHEAP
EDITED BY ROGER SHEETY
TYPESET BY GINA TALUCCI
Cover design by Joanna Williams Designs
Printed in the U.S.A.

Published articles from the *Roanoke Times* that appear in *Frugal Isn't Cheap* were written by Clare Levison between April 2009 and July 2011.

To order this title, please call toll-free 1-800-CAREER-1 (NJ and Canada: 201-848-0310) to order using VISA or MasterCard, or for further information on books from Career Press.

The Career Press, Inc.
220 West Parkway, Unit 12
Pompton Plains, NJ 07444
www.careerpress.com

Library of Congress Cataloging-in-Publication Data
Levison, Clare K.
    Frugal isn't cheap : spend less, save more, and live better / by Clare K. Levison.
        pages cm
    Includes bibliographical references and index.
    ISBN 978-1-60163-260-9 -- ISBN 978-1-60163-533-4 (ebook)
1. Finance, Personal. 2. Investments. I. Title.

HG179.L4724 2013
332.024--dc23

2013012533

For Troy, Brenna, and Elise.
I live better every day because of you.

Acknowledgments

The publication of this book has transformed a lifelong dream into reality. It has reminded me to never give up because just at the moment when you've decided it might be time to throw in the towel, everything can change. My older daughter was discussing her dreams and aspirations with me the other day. She asked, "Do you really think I could do it?" My answer is a resounding yes. Brenna, I really believe anything is possible. I don't just think, I know, you can accomplish whatever you put your mind to.

I'd like to thank Drs. Wayne and Lynn Saubert who provided me with the career guidance that resulted in the attainment of my CPA license. Their advice altered my life in ways I'm sure they never could have anticipated. I had no idea at the time where it would take me, either; not only did it lead me to a fulfilling career, it also led me to the job where I would meet my extraordinary husband.

Thank you, Troy, for being my biggest fan and loudest cheerleader; I'm so lucky that I found you, and I'm so happy that I have your loyalty and love. Thank you to my daughters, Brenna and Elise, for each being you. Brenna, you are such a strong and powerful girl. Elise, you'll always be my "tootie." I adore you both and I strive to be a mother you can be proud of.

My father instilled frugality in me from a very young age. As my uncle says, "It's the family way." He also served as my unofficial editor. Nothing went to Career Press until it went to Dad first. My mother can be summed up in seven words: eternal nurturer, continual giver, and veritable saint. Thank you both.

Close friends are so important to me. Thank you to my friends for your encouragement and interest.

Sharon Lechter is an amazingly accomplished woman, entrepreneur, writer, and CPA. Thank you, Sharon, for all your help. It's an honor to work with you.

There is such a remarkable staff at both the American Institute of Certified Public Accountants (AICPA) and the Virginia Society of Certified Public Accountants (VSCPA). Thank you for giving me the opportunity to be a volunteer. I've had the most wonderful experiences and met the most delightful people through my work with your organizations. Thank you to all my fellow AICPA National CPA Financial Literacy Commission members for your support.

My agent, Cynthia Zigmund, was committed to finding a home for this project, and her advice throughout this process has been invaluable. Thank you for believing in me and this book.

Thank you to Career Press for taking a chance on a first-time author.

I'm so grateful to have the opportunity to share my frugal message. My greatest accomplishments don't have anything to do with possessions. My greatest accomplishments will always be wife, mother, friend, and CPA.

Contents

Foreword   **17**

Introduction   **21**

1 • Living Well on Less   25

A lesson in finance from my personal trainer   *25*

Find your frugal side   *28*

Make frequent use of the words "I'd rather"   *34*

It's about your mind, not your money   *38*

Surround yourself with positive people   *40*

2 • Less Spending, More Balancing   43

*A lesson in budgeting from a
tyrannical toddler*   *43*

*Create a balanced budget using
"I have to" and "I'd rather"*   *47*

Trim your budget   *49*

*Use online banking to implement
your budget*   *60*

Be assertive about your budget   *63*

Staying on budget during the holidays   *66*

A word about Christmas   *68*

3 • Getting Out of Debt   73

A lesson in debt from Sharon Lechter   *73*

Use credit cards wisely   *77*

Check and repair your credit report   *80*

4 • Save, Save, and Save Some More   83

A lesson in savings from my golf pro   *83*

The savings challenge: 20 percent   *87*

The three-phase savings plan   *87*

Other savings opportunities   *95*

5 • Creating an Investment Plan That
   Works for You   99

    A lesson in investing from my two alpacas   *99*

    The importance of financial education   *102*

    Put the "I" back in investing   *104*

    401(k)s and IRAs   *107*

    *Employee Stock Purchase Plans and
   stock trading accounts*   *110*

    Real estate   *114*

6 • How to Make Those Large Purchases Work   117

    *A lesson in home buying from
   my days at the lake*   *117*

    *The key to a solid home investment:
   differentiation*   *120*

    Being realistic when buying a home   *122*

    The 15-year mortgage   *123*

    Buying a vehicle   *126*

    Vacations   *127*

    Everything is negotiable   *128*

7 • What Is Net Worth, and
Why Should You Care?   131

A lesson in net worth from Thomas Jefferson   *131*

*What Thomas Jefferson and MC Hammer
have in common*   *136*

The nuts and bolts of net worth   *139*

Your greatest asset, your greatest liability *147*

8 • Income: a Crucial Part of the
Financial Equation   151

*A lesson in income from my chicken
farming days*   *151*

Detrimental career profiles   *156*

Network   *162*

Your spouse's income   *163*

Alternative ways to increase your income   *164*

9 • Wanting to Be Rich Doesn't Make You Evil   167

*A lesson about the quest from
corporate America*   *167*

Money: The root of all evil?   *171*

Using money for charity   174

Charity begins at home   175

*Volunteer: give your time instead
of your money*   177

Donating small dollars   179

Donating larger dollars   181

10 • What You Should Teach Your Children   187

*A lesson about children from a
Disney princess*   187

*Should your children know how
much you have?*   189

Plant the seed of frugality   192

*Allowances, budget money, and paying
for grades*   194

Keeping up with the Joneses, college style   200

Set a good example   204

11 • Achieving Financial Success   207

The simple formula   207

Commit to the mental shift   209

Incorporate change in to your daily life   *210*

Put it all together   *212*

Live better   *215*

Notes   **219**

Index   **227**

About the Author   **233**

Foreword

When it comes to money, you have a choice. You can become a master of or a slave to your money. In *Frugal Isn't Cheap*, Clare Levison highlights the importance of the choices you make each and every day. Will you choose to live beyond your means and mortgage your future with high amounts of debt? Or will you live within your means and become the master of your money and therefore the master of your destiny?

Personal finance does not need to be complicated and learning how to secure your financial wealth doesn't need to be boring. Through her real-life stories about money, Clare shares her journey of becoming a financial literacy expert with humor and compassion, and even through a few tears. The best way to learn anything is through real-life experience. By sharing the learning opportunities she had along the way, Clare strives to spare you from having to repeat the mistakes of so many others in your own financial life.

Being financially savvy has never been more important. Young people are graduating from college with large school loans and, unable to immediately find jobs, often begin their careers already enslaved by debt. According to both the Center for American Progress and the Consumer Financial Protection Bureau, student debt now exceeds $1 trillion ($864 billion in federal loans and $150 billion in private loans). This problem is intensified when these young people enter the work force and are not able to find jobs. According to a 2012 investigation by the Associated Press, more than 50 percent of recent graduates are still unemployed or under-employed.

The need for financial education was made clear to me when my oldest son went off to college years ago. He came home for the holidays already $2,500 in credit card debt! It was quite obvious that he had truly enjoyed his first semester of college until the bills were due. I was very angry at him, but I was even angrier with myself. I had taught my son about money, but apparently I hadn't taught him successfully about the perils of credit card debt. He was often with me when I used my credit cards, but not when I paid them off each month. We refused to bail him out financially, and he started his own seven-year journey to get out of debt and repair his credit rating. Like Clare, he often shares his story so that others can learn from his mistakes and learning opportunities. My experience with my son created the tremendous passion that I still have for highlighting the need for financial literacy.

Ensuring that the current generations of teens and young adults have a financial education is essential to the financial stability of our families and our country. The gift of a financial education is the gift of a lifetime and will allow young people to not just survive, but to thrive in the economy they will face as adults.

Whether it is Clare's stories or the lessons you have learned from your own money mistakes, the message is quite simple: Spend less than you earn. By following this simple mantra, you will become a master of your money and create a financial foundation of security for you and your family while discovering today's new money reality. Being frugal can be the new "cool."

Seize the opportunity today to become smart with your money and become financially independent while still having fun and enjoying life. Will you be a master of your money or a slave to it? It truly is your choice.

All the best,
Sharon Lechter, CPA, CGMA
Coauthor of *Rich Dad Poor Dad* and *Think and Grow Rich—Three Feet from Gold*, annotator of *Outwitting the Devil* with the Napoleon Hill Foundation, author of *Save Wisely, Spend Happily*, founder and CEO of Pay Your Family First, creator of the award-winning *Thrive Time for Teens* board game, member of the first President's Advisory Council on Financial Literacy, and member of the AICPA's National CPA Financial Literacy Commission

Introduction

I sat down at my computer last week to do some online banking. I went to my bank's Website, put in my username and password, and hit the enter key. I nearly fell out of my chair when I saw what came up on the screen in front of me. I was in the red—negative. I had overdrawn my account.

"How can this be?" I thought to myself. I normally check my online banking every day. It's something I think everyone should do. But I had gotten busy, so it had been a few days since my last log-in. After some quick analysis I realized a withdrawal had posted a day earlier than I was expecting, a day earlier than my deposit. This bad timing had started a chain of events that wreaked havoc on my account. It was my own fault. I should have been paying closer attention. I shouldn't have been cutting it so close. There was nobody to blame but me.

I was mortified. I know better. I'm a CPA, for crying out loud—a finance expert. I extol the virtues of being financially responsible, yet I had screwed up. I felt hypocritical; I felt embarrassed; I felt human.

Keeping your finances in order isn't always easy; it requires continual effort and vigilance. Just like any other self-improvement effort such as dieting, exercising, or keeping a clean and organized home, it requires discipline. And often discipline is not a lot of fun. There may be a million other things you'd rather be doing, but still you have to take time to take care of your finances. So I picked myself up off the floor, gave myself forty lashes with a wet noodle—I deserved every last one of them—and got back to business. And that's what you should do, too.

If you're one of the many Americans whose finances are in disorder, if you've lost your job, if you've lost your home, if you have a mountain of debt or a mole hill of savings, pick yourself up and get back to business. Those negative emotions you've felt over your financial situation can spur you on and make you stronger. They can help ensure you remain vigilant and don't backslide into financial turmoil again.

Don't spend time trying to find someone else to blame. Don't create a long list of excuses for why you haven't taken control of your financial future. Yes, you should have been making the mortgage payment on time every month.

Yes, you should have started saving with the first paycheck you ever brought home. Yes, you should have created a balanced budget and paid for your purchases rather than charging them to a credit card. But if you didn't, do it now.

A Chinese proverb says: "The best time to plant a tree was twenty years ago. The second best time, is today." If your finances aren't in the condition that they should be, then start cleaning them up. Start today.

1

Living Well on Less

A lesson in finance from my personal trainer

I always had it in the back of my mind that when my younger daughter went to kindergarten, I was going to get a personal trainer. I figured now that the baby was five and a half years old, I could no longer continue to claim that my extra flab was post-pregnancy related. When the day came, I sent my little dear out the door and headed off to the local gym.

I was expecting to walk in there, do a few leg presses, a few crunches, maybe a lunge or two, and walk out looking like I was 18 again. So I was pretty disappointed when I made a total fool of myself flopping around on the stability ball, leg pressed until my thighs burned, did about 75 lunges, and walked out looking exactly the same as when I went in, except I was a lot sweatier and my hair was a wreck.

"This really sucks," I thought, as I threw myself down on the couch to recover the minute I got home, and it did. That night I woke up repeatedly with the feeling that someone was trying to rip my arms off, and the next day I could barely move. But what sucked even more was my realization that this was not going to be quick, and it was not going to be easy. There is no miracle cure for cellulite. I realized the first step was to face that reality, meet it head on, and then continue my journey.

Obviously, you're reading this book because you want to improve yourself financially. It's my job to help you do that, and the first step is exactly the same as the one just mentioned: a little dose of reality. There is no miracle cure for your finances. There is no quick, easy way to get rich. I'm not going to promise that you can read this book and become a double-digit millionaire, just like my trainer couldn't promise that I'd leave the gym with six-pack abs, but that's okay. The good news is that with persistence and effort, you can achieve your financial goals.

The other day a friend of mine was going through some of her old memorabilia and came across some pictures of our children when they graduated from preschool together. She scanned a picture of my older daughter and sent it to me along with a quote of what my daughter said she had learned in preschool: "Don't pull people if they don't want to go."

I don't want to pull you down your financial path kicking and screaming. I want you to walk with me. I don't want to lecture you or make you feel guilty. I want you to have a successful financial future, not because I'm telling you to, but because you want to. I don't want you to abstain from spending but rather to do so responsibly by putting more of your money into things that are going to help you build wealth. The choice is yours. You can either come up with all kinds of reasons why you can't make changes to your finances, or you can come up with all kinds of reasons why you will make changes to your finances.

I'm a big believer in the KISS principle: Keep It Simple, Stupid. However, as a southern gal, I find "Stupid" to be a little harsh. So I prefer to follow the KISH principle: Keep It Simple, Honey. In the pages that follow, you'll find simple advice that regular people, like you and me, can use to improve our finances. Hopefully, this advice will shed some light on how you may be flushing your money down the toilet instead of funneling it into your savings or investment accounts, and how you can best use your money to build wealth. I've also included some "Do the Math" equations that will help illustrate the financial concepts discussed.

Your next step on this journey will be to find your frugal side, so I've included some "Frugal Homework" in this chapter. I want to change the way you think about money because I can promise that, if you can and then apply those changes to the financial choices you make, you can create a secure and bright financial future for yourself. If you can change your outlook one step at a time, you'll truly change your life. So without further ado, let's get to it.

Find your frugal side

When I was growing up, I can remember complaining to my dad about it being cold in the house. Truth be told, it was probably plenty warm for most people, but I've always been cold natured. "Go put a sweater on," he would tell me. Dad's always been a frugal man.

But today's society has become obsessed with excess. Frugal people are seen as dull and boring. Big spenders seem flashy and exciting. However, I think the tide is finally beginning to turn on these perceptions. And that's a good thing. It's just not fashionable to own 20 pairs of shoes that you've only worn once. It's not cool to have 30 gadgets that you never use. And if you're spending all your money on designer clothes, you're not stylish; you're silly. Now more than ever, frugality is coming into fashion, and it's hip to be thrifty. It turns out Dad was frugal before frugal was cool.

Do the math

According to a *ShopSmart* magazine survey,[1] women are willing to spend an average of $49 per pair of shoes and own an average of 17 pairs. That's $833 sitting in the closet! The average person's unused gadget list might include a

Wine Aerator—$39; FryDaddy (thank your lucky stars that you're not using this one)—$30; Workout Equipment (just in case you decide to use the FryDaddy)—$100. That's $169 and probably just the tip of the iceberg on your useless gadget collection. If you owned half as many shoes and skipped the gadgets altogether, the money in your bank account would total $585.50.

If I had to come up with one synonym for frugal, it wouldn't be "cheap"; it would be "smart." Being frugal isn't about buying the cheapest thing; it's about buying the things that are truly a good value. Let me put it to you another way. You have to start spending less, so you can have more. Many things like cars, clothes, and furniture depreciate greatly the minute you take them home. You need to think hard before spending a lot on those kinds of purchases. Look for bargains, buy used, and don't be ashamed to shop at discount stores. Put more of your money into things that are going to appreciate. For example:

$ Price of a solid wood coffee table and two end tables, new, purchased from a furniture store—$299.

$ Price of a solid wood coffee table and two end tables, three years old, purchased on Craigslist—$75.

$ Money in your bank account—$224.

I'm amazed that some people can spend hundreds, even thousands, of dollars each month on clothes. The next time you're tempted to go on a shopping spree, remember: As soon as you wear that designer shirt once, it's worth a fraction of what you spent on it. Kind of ironic, isn't it? You pay top dollar to a big corporation just so you can clip that tag. Not only that, but every time you wear the shirt, the corporation is getting free advertising.

I was doing some shopping at a discount store one day and happened to pick up a white cardigan for $15. It quickly became one of my favorite sweaters, and I wore it frequently. On at least two separate occasions, I was told how cute it was. One of the women who complimented me also mentioned that she had seen it at a designer store and admired it. Obviously, she couldn't tell the difference between the discount sweater and the designer one. Designer store price: $75. Money in my bank account: $60.

We all like to have nice things. For me there's no substitute for a high-quality blazer—the perfect cut and quality fabric are worth every penny. But there's a limit. I'm not suggesting that you should forgo all the frills in life, but aren't a couple of nice dresses and suits enough? Do you really need 10 handbags, or would two or three be perfectly adequate? If your closet is so crammed full that you could clothe the entire neighborhood, there's a problem and it goes deeper than money. Clothing is just one example, but it demonstrates well the concern so many people have with looking good on the outside, even though they're falling apart financially behind closed doors.

Frugal people don't spend their time wishing they had more stuff. They avoid excess. In fact, they take pride in being understated with their possessions. You have to nurture that mentality within yourself. You aren't what you own. Being secure with who you are is one of the most important factors in financial success. If you don't have self-confidence, you'll constantly be comparing yourself to others. If you're not self-assured, you leave yourself vulnerable to the "keeping up with the Joneses" mentality.

Does your financial life consist of smoke and mirrors rather than dollars and cents? Have you found yourself with a solid credit card bill instead of a solid savings account? Do others view you as well-to-do, even though you're barely squeaking by? If your answer to any of these questions is yes, you are not alone. Many people these days are living a lifestyle that can only be described as "all hat, no cattle." They're putting on a good show, but they don't really have the financial resources to be living the lifestyle they are. They've got champagne taste on a beer budget.

I guess I'm just a simple country girl, but big houses, fancy cars, and designer labels don't impress me. If you have a chalet in Aspen or a house on the waterway in Ft. Lauderdale, I'd love to come for a visit but I'll let you keep the mortgage. I can't remember the last time I drove a new car. Right now I've got an SUV with more than 135,000 miles on it, but it gets me where I need to go most of the time. And although I have been known to buy a designer purse or two, it's always at the outlet. Believe it or not, I prefer it that way.

I watched a show once about a single woman raising her two grandchildren, ages 3 and 7. She would drop them off at daycare and school each morning, go to work as a waitress and bartender all day, then go home and do homework with them in the evening. That impresses me.

If your financial life is a fake, the only one you're fooling is you. Do you want to surround yourself with people who put the most value on material possessions? I prefer those who find hard work, responsibility, and integrity to be the things of greatest importance. Financial exaggeration is usually just a thin disguise for insecurity, emptiness, and self-doubt. If you've been feeling the need to overinflate your financial standing, what you need to start doing instead is nurturing your frugal side. Maybe you need to get a new group of friends, or maybe you need to get a new budget. Flashiness fades, but broke is forever. I don't know about you, but I'd take a herd of cattle over a big hat any day.

Frugal homework

Make a list of the best qualities you possess as a person. You might describe yourself as:

1. A good mother/father.
2. A loving husband/wife.
3. A competent teacher/nurse/auto mechanic.
4. Neat and clean.
5. Stylish.

Now, make a list of your most important possessions. Your list might include your:

1. House.
2. Car.

3. Jewelry.
4. Clothes.
5. Big-screen TV.

These are the physical things that are a part of your life, but they are not a part of your character. You need to see that the first list—the qualities about you that make you who you are—stands on its own. It's static, even as your list of physical possessions is dynamic. If you are neat, clean, and stylish, that doesn't change. I would put all of those qualities on my list, and I feel confident that I'm going to look just as good in a $15 discount store sweater as I would in one that's designer. If you are neat, clean, and stylish, your home will reflect that. You don't need a house that's 4,000 square feet to show who you are. Your tidy, well-organized space can be just as enjoyable and stylish at half that size.

I have a friend who went through that exact scenario. She and her husband decided it was time to downsize. They sold their very large, customized home and bought a smaller, more standard version. I was shocked when they told me about the move. Their sprawling brick home was just gorgeous—flawlessly furnished and decorated, spotlessly maintained. It was so enjoyable to eat dinner at their house and relax on the back patio. I have to admit, I thought they were a little nuts to be giving all that up.

But as soon as I stepped into their new home for the first time, I realized I was the one who hadn't been able to see the bigger picture. Their smaller home was just as gorgeous. Even without the large foyer and vaulted ceilings, this home gave an immediate feeling of elegance. The physical things were different, but the characteristics of the owners were still the same. My friend has fabulous taste and style, and that hadn't changed. Because of who she is as a person, she was able to make her smaller space look every bit as fabulous as the larger one had. She's also an excellent cook. Sure, she might have given up her stainless steel kitchen, but the food that came out of her mid-grade oven was every bit as tasty as it had always been, and we ate, drank wine, and laughed just as hard on her new smaller patio.

Make frequent use of the words "I'd rather"

Frugal people don't derive pleasure from having the newest model vehicle or the biggest house on the block. Their enjoyment comes from knowing they have a secure financial future. Frugal people know something their non-frugal peers haven't figured out yet: Each dollar spent is a dollar that could have been invested.

I want you to stop being concerned about keeping up with the Joneses and start making frequent use of the words "I'd rather." Let's say you're talking with your neighbors who just bought a brand-new ski boat. They're very excited about taking it out for the first cruise of the summer. Because they know how much you love the water, they suggest that you should look into getting a boat too. What do you do?

First, resist the urge to hop in the car, drive to the nearest boat lot, and buy one that's got more horsepower than your neighbor's. Then say something like, "I love your boat. I'm sure it's going to be lots of fun, but I'd rather save up for the kids' college tuition. I don't want them to have to take out any student loans."

Do the math

Going out on your neighbor's boat with them: Free. That's called out-smarting the Joneses.

"I'd rather" is empowering. "I'd rather" says: I have choices and I'm making smart decisions. I'm not comparing myself to my friends or neighbors or coworkers. I'm not influenced by their decisions. I'm the captain of my financial ship. I'm in control.

When it comes to spending, remember you have nothing to prove to the rest of the world. Prove to yourself that you can be smart with your money. Make "I'd rather" a part of your daily life. Wouldn't you rather be debt free and sitting on a good nest egg?

Frugal homework

Here's another exercise that will help strengthen your frugal mind. I call it the Bargain Brand Challenge.

I'm always amazed at the money people will spend needlessly just because they're worried about looking cheap. While on a recent vacation, I had a conversation with a bus driver about the different hotels available around the area where we were staying. She cautioned me not to stay at certain more expensive hotels, because they were no better than their less expensive counterparts.

As strange as it sounds, companies realize that some people actually like paying more for things. It makes them feel important, a step above the rest of the crowd. They assume they must be getting more because they're paying more, but that's an incorrect assumption.

The bus driver had it figured out, but lots of people don't. Name-brand Nancy or name-brand Ned, as the case may be, won't buy anything that doesn't have that well-recognized symbol or registered trademark. For them, everything from hand lotion to hotels must be top of the line, the latest and greatest. No less than the (perceived) best will do.

But is that little symbol really worth those extra dollars? Does more expensive really mean better? Are you guilty of buying higher-priced things just because you think someone else will view them as better?

I'm challenging you, for one week, to choose one of the least expensive options available whenever you make a purchase. For example, if you need a box of cereal, buy the generic.

Do the math

$ Price of a box of name-brand raisin bran—$3.09.

$ Price of a box of generic raisin bran—$0.99.

$ Difference—$2.10.

$ Savings if you purchased one box per week—52 x $2.10, or $109.20 per year.

$ If you want to watch a movie, rent a DVD.

$ Cost to take a family of four to the movie theater—
4 x $10, or $40.

$ Cost for a family of four to watch a movie rented
from Redbox—$1.

$ Money in your bank account—$39.

I guarantee you'll find that lots of less expensive things
are just as good as their higher-priced counterparts. For
some things, you'll decide the more expensive items really
are higher quality and therefore worth the extra money.
But you'll never know unless you explore all your lower
cost options.

I'm not suggesting that buying cheap cheese or inexpensive ice cream is going to take you straight to the fin-
ish line of financial success. I'm not even suggesting you'll
want to buy cheap cheese. I personally find that cheese
in a can to be barely edible. What I am saying is that you
need to buy the items that represent the best value for your
money. If you buy something that costs less and tastes terrible, no one will eat it and you'll end up throwing it out.
That's not a good value. On the other hand, if you pay extra for a name brand that's no tastier than a less expensive
version, that's not a good value, either.

Examining the value in the little purchases you make
will help you begin training your mind for life's financial
marathon. Start small. Twenty-five cents off of toilet paper
may not seem like a big deal, but eventually it'll add up,

because your new frugal thinking will begin to expand to larger purchases. Suddenly you'll be shopping for a used car instead of new. You'll be looking for a home that has the features you need in a price range you can easily afford. Those things will have a huge impact on your financial future.

It's about your mind, not your money

Being frugal is a state of mind. Frugal people are very conscious of each dollar they spend. They have a heightened awareness during the spending process. They don't just swipe their credit or debit card blindly. They put thought into each transaction.

That's why, believe it or not, I'm not going to tell you to cut up all your credit cards or stop using your debit cards. Those things are merely the vehicle through which you do your spending. I hate to tell you this, but if you are in debt, your credit card is not the problem. Your lack of frugality is. If your checking account is constantly overdrawn, it's not the debit card's fault; it's yours.

Many people believe that credit and debit cards have replaced paper money as the root of all evil. In today's economy, credit cards have come to represent debt, and debit cards have come to represent mindless spending. What I believe credit and debit cards represent is technological advancement. If you have the right money mentality, a piece of plastic can't hurt you. (In fact, with points for cash back, free hotel rooms, and so forth, it can actually help you). But if you have the wrong money mentality, your finances will be in disorder no matter what kind of financial instruments you use.

To put the majority of the blame on the credit card companies or banks is a terrible mistake. Sure, both have engaged in some questionable practices, and in those cases, they do need to be reined in. But what happened to personal responsibility? Our country was founded on the principles of freedom, and we all know that with freedom comes great responsibility. That's why frugal people consistently employ the concept of "just because I can, doesn't mean I should."

When my friends put their large, extravagant home on the market, I thought to myself, "Why are they doing that? They can afford that home. So what if the maintenance costs more, big deal if the utility bills are higher. They can afford it." What I failed to see was that just because they could didn't mean they should. Their kids had gone off to college, and they didn't need all that space anymore. They had gotten a new dog and wanted a bigger yard. Their priorities had changed. Even though they could afford it, it wasn't the best use of their money. In fact, it had become a waste, and frugal people strongly disapprove of waste.

Embracing the "just because I can, doesn't mean I should" concept is a key part of developing a new, more frugal mindset. I also want to stress this slight variation: Just because someone else will let me, doesn't mean I should. This is going to be particularly crucial if you choose to hang on to those credit and debit cards. Just because Mr. Major Credit Card Company will give you a $25,000 limit, doesn't mean you should use it, and just because Mrs. Major Bank will give you overdraft protection of $1,000, doesn't mean you should use that, either.

If you can become more aware of your spending and begin to believe that it's better done in moderation, if you begin to pay closer attention to each money choice you make, if you find and nurture your frugal side, you have taken big steps toward a successful financial future.

Surround yourself with positive people

Every year people make their New Year's resolutions. Going to the gym, getting the house organized, and spending less are some of the standards. Perhaps you bought this book because it was your New Year's resolution to get your finances in order. But frequently after a few months, or maybe even weeks, the resolutions become too difficult to keep. Extra pounds return, extra dollars get spent, and that storage room in the basement never does get cleaned out. It's such an established pattern, that one might say New Year's resolutions are made to be broken. Why is this the case so many times? The resolution is typically an admirable one that would be of great benefit if kept. Yet, it is still too hard to follow through.

One of the reasons is that resolutions are often too broad. To be successful, you have to set specific goals. Let me suggest a specific goal you should embrace in your quest to live more frugally: I will surround myself with people that want to see me succeed. Sounds simple enough, doesn't it? But one of the sad realities of our society is that often people find it difficult to stomach others' success and easy to revel in their failure.

You needn't look any further than the Tiger Woods infidelity incident to know this is true. I'm not saying that what Tiger did wasn't wrong. What I am saying is that the glee with which the media reported on his fall from grace was pretty apparent. People love to see success turn into failure. I suppose with celebrities, it just comes with the territory. Hopefully in your own life, you can find it easier to surround yourself with people who take a genuine interest in you and your success. More than likely, you already have a good idea who these people are and who they aren't.

The world can be a cold place. Jealousy, pessimism, and negative gossip seem to spread more quickly and with more gusto than kindness and optimism. But it's much warmer when you find those who are interested in lifting you up rather than tearing you down.

Encircle yourself with positive people. Ask for help when you need it, and reciprocate the support and encouragement you receive. Living more frugally is about your mind, not your money. There is no quick-fix, but the effort you put in will be well worth it. Embrace frugality, embrace "I'd rather," and embrace those who want to see you succeed.

2

Less Spending, More Balancing

A lesson in budgeting from a tyrannical toddler

When my younger daughter was 5, clearly past the toddler stage in years but not always in behavior, her tantrums began escalating in frequency and intensity. Bedtime became a true nightmare. Every night, my husband and I would brace ourselves for the fight. As soon as I would say, "It's bedtime," the screaming, crying, and gnashing of teeth would begin. My daughter didn't want to sleep in her own bed. In fact, she didn't want to go to bed at all. What she really wanted was to stay up and party all night long, all the while becoming more cranky and inconsolable with every passing minute.

What my daughter hated second only to bedtime was being told no. "Can we do spin art, Mommy?" she might ask. An answer of "No, I don't think we're going to get that out right now" would result in an immediate backlash. "But whyyy?" she would moan and then throw herself onto the floor and begin rolling around as if the injustice of it all was so great that she couldn't even endure standing upright.

My husband, my older daughter, and I began feeling like we were being held hostage. We walked on eggshells around her. We did what we could to appease her so we wouldn't have to listen to the loud, unpleasant tantrums. Sometimes nothing we did would work, at which point my husband and older daughter would typically flee the scene to another room and leave me to deal with my little darling.

As things continued, I began feeling what I imagine women throughout the ages have felt when things aren't going right in their household: guilt. I questioned myself: Had I given her too much? Had I spoiled her? She is the baby. Maybe I had ruined her for life by treating her like one. Then again, maybe I hadn't given her enough. I had been working on some extra projects, and maybe I hadn't been giving her the quality time she needed. Maybe this was her way of acting out.

Either way, the tantrums continued but they were pretty much confined to the walls of our own home. At school, she was an angel. Her teacher remarked at our conference that if all the children in the class were like my daughter, her job would be easy. I wondered if we were talking about the same kid, but I said nothing, thankful that at least my daughter's wrath only came down on those of us in the family.

Then one fateful day it happened. I pulled up to the school to drop my daughter off, and she wouldn't get out of the car. She launched into one of her fits, and I had to pry her out of the backseat and drag her into the building. Her teacher looked so surprised to see her crying and me clearly flustered. "I think we're just having a bad morning," I said sheepishly. Then I got in the car and did two things. The first was to cry myself. The second was to decide that this had absolutely gone too far. Things had reached an all-time low. I needed a plan and I needed to implement it swiftly.

I think I'm a pretty great mom, but this problem had presented me with a behavior challenge that I hadn't experienced in my parenting up to that point. In the moment, it had seemed easier for me to try to appease her so the tantrum would stop quickly. Sometimes it worked and sometimes it didn't, but it clearly wasn't getting me anywhere in the long run.

I didn't need to beat myself up. What I needed to do was be firm, and I needed to do it consistently. But being firm can be hard work. What I realized was that I had known in my heart all along what needed to be done. I just hadn't done it.

That afternoon I informed my daughter that because of her behavior she was losing her outside play privileges and would be helping me with the laundry instead. This, of course, started a huge tantrum, but I held firm, and my older daughter went out to play while the younger one helped me put clothes into the washing machine. I informed her that this would be the way things went until the tantrums stopped. It took a few days, but stop they did.

My daughter is a few years older now, and her behavior at home has continued to improve greatly over time. It's almost hard for me to remember how truly difficult those tantrum days were. Honestly, I don't know how much of the turnaround is attributable to my fabulous parenting and how much of it is attributable to Mother Nature, because I'm sure part of it is just due to the fact that she got older and grew out of it.

Maybe you've had an embarrassing money moment that caused you to reevaluate your finances. Maybe you bounced a check or had your credit or debit card declined. Perhaps it was even more serious, and you had your home foreclosed or had to file for bankruptcy. Or maybe it's just time for you to grow out of your haphazard money management ways. Putting discipline into your finances might not be a lot of fun. Neither is disciplining your children. But when you reach the point that you know it must be done (and I'm assuming you've reached that point because you're reading this book), you will find the motivation to do it. I'm not saying it's always going to be easy, but hopefully I can convince you that most of the time it doesn't have to be horribly difficult. It's time to put your foot down when it comes to your finances. It's time to say, "I've had enough. This is it. This has gone too far."

Create a balanced budget using "I have to" and "I'd rather"

If there's one cardinal rule of budgeting, it's this: Don't spend more than you make. Sounds simple, doesn't it? But the average American family spends $1.22 for every $1 it earns.[1] Your goal should be to create a balanced budget. Even though the government can't seem to do it, you can. When doing so, remember these two phrases: "I have to" and "I'd rather."

First, write down your monthly take-home pay after taxes and insurance; even better, put it into a spreadsheet program like Microsoft Excel. Then, write down all of your monthly bills that fall into the "I have to" category. This should include things like the payment on a mortgage you've taken out or an apartment lease you've signed. Payments on car, student, or credit card loans, and utility and medical bills would be other examples. In reality, very few things in life are true "I have to's," but for the purposes of this exercise, we're going to put anything where the money has already been committed and you have to make good on payment into this category.

If you subtract your "I have to's" from your take-home income, you will know how much you have left for the "I'd rathers." This category includes all your other expenses, such as groceries, gas, clothing, and entertainment. But wait—aren't groceries and gas "I have to's"? You have to eat. You have to put gas in your tank in order to get to work. But you do have choices about what to buy. Would you rather buy the name-brand cereal or the generic? Would you rather drive an SUV or an economy car? Savings also falls into this category. Would you rather take a trip to Europe or save that money for a real estate investment? (In the next chapter, I'll discuss how much you should be putting into savings, but here's a sneak peak. The figure I have in mind is 20 percent.) For the purposes of this exercise, we're going to put anything where the money has not yet been committed into this category.

Here's the result you're looking for: Take-home pay minus "I have to's" minus "I'd rathers" equals zero. This is a balanced budget.

Here's the result you might get: Take-home pay minus "I have to's" minus "I'd rathers" equals a negative number. This is a deficit.

If you have a deficit, you'll need to trim your expenses, not only to get your budget balanced but also to carve out enough for savings. Here's the bottom line: Budgeting is all about making choices. You have a pot of money (your income), and you get to choose how you want to divvy it out each month. Divvying out more than what is in the pot is not a choice. You can't buy things you can't pay for—period. Stop considering credit cards as an option, unless you can pay them off each month. Stop borrowing against your home for day-to-day expenditures. And for heaven's sake, don't even consider one of those quick cash places. There are only two ways you can truly balance your household budget: spend less or make more. Anything else is merely living above your means.

Creating a balanced budget is an essential part of managing your household finances, but it's a task many people don't enjoy. They view it as tedious or intimidating, and about as exciting as watching paint dry. Budgeting reminds us that our money is not unlimited, and that's a message we'd often like to do without. But given the current state of the economy, it's one that should be shouted from the roof tops. You don't have the right to buy a $500,000 house if you don't have the income to make the monthly payments. You do have the responsibility to manage your finances in such a way that they do not become a burden on your own family or the rest of society.

By the way, if you do this exercise and get this result, take-home pay minus "I have to's" minus "I'd rathers" equals a positive number, then you have a surplus. Congratulations! However, you want to be sure every dollar has a home. You don't want the extra money just sitting around in your checking account where you'll be tempted to spend it. You want it funneled into savings instead. And remember that even if your preliminary calculations show that you have a balanced budget or even a surplus, you may still need to do some trimming in order to carve out enough for savings.

Trim your budget

Trimming your budget may seem overwhelming. I believe this is largely due to the fact that we've convinced ourselves that so many of the luxuries in life are actually necessities. Here are just a few examples.

Satellite or cable TV and phone service

How does $65 per month turn into $135? I don't know, but ask the satellite companies; they can tell you. The add-ons to turn your home into a home theater can really add up: 250 channels, in HD of course, and that doesn't include the movie channels and the charges for extra receivers and DVRs. Good grief. Aren't 120 regular old non-HD channels more than enough? By the way, my husband will be vigorously shaking his head no as he reads this.

I don't know if the phone companies took a lesson from the satellite companies or vice versa, but they're clearly playing the same game: unlimited talk, unlimited text, and unlimited data. The only thing limited here is your bank account. And they stick it to you twice: once for a cell phone (for you and every other member of your family) and again for a land line.

Groceries

You've probably noticed that the price of food is on the rise. This includes everything from dairy to meat to produce. There are several reasons contributing to these increases. The first is extreme weather, such as droughts. Extreme weather causes damage to crops, which in turn causes supply to go down and prices to go up. In addition, there's an increasing demand for food worldwide due to growing populations.

Growth in biofuels, such as ethanol, has also increased the demand for corn. Corn is in approximately 75 percent of all processed foods in the grocery store, so the increased demand for corn causes an increase in the price of all kinds of foods.[2] Increased oil prices have also driven up the cost of transportation, which drives up food price.

Still, I always wonder what the people who say they can't feed their family for a reasonable amount of money are buying for dinner. If you're tightening your budget it's time to trade the steak for Spam and the mussels for mac and cheese. Okay, maybe Spam is pushing it, but you get the idea. Plenty of meals are well-balanced and low-cost, and there are entire Websites devoted to giving you low-cost recipe ideas in case you tire of the ever-popular spaghetti and meat sauce or hamburgers and french fries.

Here are a few tips to help you stay on budget at the grocery store:

$ Get a grocery store discount card. It's free and good for reduced prices and special sales at that particular store. Some cards even accrue points that can be used for discounts on other things such as gas.

$ Make a shopping list and stick to it. If you go to the grocery store without a list, you'll be more likely to make impulse purchases and spend more money than necessary. Get your children involved in helping to make the list and let them know that's all you're buying. This way they'll be less likely to beg for extras once you get to the store.

$ Don't put extra junk food on the list. Sticking to the items for three meals and two small snacks per day can also help you stick to your budget.

$ Plan your menu for the week based on what's on sale at the grocery store that week. Use the sale flyer to help you make your shopping list.

$ Look online for low-cost recipes. Remember to search for recipes that use ingredients that are on sale at your grocery store that week.

$ Buy in bulk for staple items that you use all the time. Buy reasonable quantities for the size of your family (not a five-year supply, but a one- to three-month supply).

$ Take dinner leftovers for lunch the next day. This can be a healthier and less expensive alternative to heating up a frozen meal, and much less expensive than eating lunch out every day.

$ Avoid products such as pre-made children's lunches and individual bags of chips. Children love these kinds of food because their packing makes them look fun and exciting, but they'll cost you a lot more than making the same lunch yourself and dividing out a large bag of chips into your own individual portions.

$ Buy generic. Take the Bargain Brand Challenge and find generic products that are a good value.

$ Use coupons, but only for things you need. Don't be tempted to buy something just because it's a good deal. Buying things you don't need is never a bargain.

Being extreme

$500 worth of groceries for $4.20. $1,000 worth of groceries for $10.39. $1,500 worth of groceries for $20.55. If you've been watching reality TV lately, you know exactly what I'm talking about: extreme couponing. Although I find it entertaining (I mean, who doesn't like to watch women dive into dumpsters to retrieve coupons for 50 cents off of croutons), I also find the concept financially flawed.

Here's the basic premise. The contestant fills several shopping carts to the brim, and heads to the checkout aisle, where the full price of the groceries is rung up. Then the coupons are scanned, and we all watch in awe as that large dollar amount drops down to next to nothing. Extreme couponers will buy anything they have a good coupon for and they always buy in large quantities. This makes the show interesting but doesn't always make good financial sense. The problem is these people are "saving" on a bunch of things they don't even like or need. Two of my favorite examples are a lady who bought about 30 bottles of mustard for her family who didn't even eat mustard and a lady who bought a ton of diapers but had no children. Clearly, these people did get free stuff, but you can only call it savings if you're getting money off of things you would have normally purchased anyway.

A friend and I recently attended an event together at a local civic center. As I turned into the parking lot, I immediately became aggravated with the fact that all of the spaces right in the front had been taken. As I weaved in and out of the rows grumbling about how long it was taking to find a space (I mean, it had been at least 30 seconds since we had pulled into the lot), my friend turned to me and said, "Is this free parking?" I looked at her confused, as she proceeded to tell me that she was used to paying quite a bit for civic center parking. My friend had just moved from the city.

I parked the car about 10 rows back, and we headed inside. Of course, the concession stand was right there to greet us, and my friend popped over to check out what they had. When she reported to me that drinks were several dollars, I responded with, "I know. It's expensive, isn't it?" She informed me that she was used to paying twice that much. It was beginning to feel like a version of the City Mouse and the Country Mouse, and we got a good laugh out of it.

But remember that although cost may be relative, common sense isn't. I had a professor in college who would say, "I'm not going to keep hitting myself in the head with a hammer, just because it'll feel really good when I stop." You're not getting more for your money when you buy things you don't need in the first place. Three dollars is still a lot to spend for a soda, even if you're used to paying six. When you're assessing your finances, you have to throw all your preconceived notions out the window. Start from scratch and see if those dollars could be put to much better use. Figure out if something makes sense on a stand-alone basis, then decide how to spend.

My second pet peeve with extreme couponing is the idea that these men and women are doing the equivalent of earning a great salary by getting all of their family's groceries for free.

Do the math

The USDA calculates the average cost of food for a home at four different levels: thrifty, low-cost, moderate-cost, and liberal.[3] Their calculations are also based on the number of people in the family. If I pick a family of four and moderate-cost, the average weekly food cost as of June 2012 is $236.60, an amount that could easily cover household items as well. Many couponers admit to spending about 30 hours per week couponing.

$236.60 divided by 30 equals $7.89 per hour, not the equivalent of a great salary, but the equivalent of a minimum wage job. All of the couponer's energy and enthusiasm channeled elsewhere could certainly earn more than that and be used for items the family actually needs.

What is the moral here? Don't be extreme; just be smart. If it won't be consumed within a reasonable time frame, don't buy it. That time frame should be about 90 days, and if you'd like to limit it to 30 or 60, even better. When it comes to coupons, clip them when they're for items you typically purchase. Otherwise, buy when things are on sale, and don't make couponing a full-time job.

Eating out

I love eating out. The amount of money I pay in restaurant bills is definitely one of the areas of my budget where there's room for quite a bit of belt tightening. If I'd stop eating out so much, I'd surely be able to literally tighten my belt another notch or two as well, but that's a subject for a different book.

Over the course of the next month, track how much you spend eating out. The result may shock you. How can you feast more frugally, have your cake and eat it too, so to speak?

$ Skip the drinks. Beverages at a restaurant, alcoholic and non-alcoholic, can be very expensive. The average price for a restaurant soda is around $2. For two adults and two children, depending on whether or not a drink is included with the children's meals (often it's not), drinks alone could end up costing you $8. You could buy eight two-liters for that. Alcoholic drinks are even more expensive. The bottom line is if you must have a soda, pour yourself a glass when you get home, and the same goes for the cocktails.

$ Skip the dessert. Just like beverages, restaurant desserts can be very expensive. Keep a stash of mini candy bars on hand and let one of those be your indulgence after your meal.

$ Skip the appetizer. Are you sensing a theme here? Don't order the extras. Forget about all the add-ons. Lots of places will bring free bread or chips anyway.

$ Split a meal. Portions these days are so large you can often easily share a meal and still get full, and you'll save some dollars to boot.

$ Go to kids' night. If you have children, many restaurants have a kids eat free night. Children's meals can be costly, so frequenting kids' night can save quite a few bucks.

Entertainment

This category is full of indulgences, but a wise person once said, "The best things in life are free." Embrace this concept whole-heartedly. To stay on budget, start focusing on the fact that quality time doesn't have to be costly. Libraries, parks, and good old-fashioned conversations are all free, and they can enhance your life in just as many ways as expensive entertainment. Make a list of all the activities you can do, either by yourself or with your friends or family members, that are free, such as taking a walk, riding a bike, or playing a board game. Then when you feel the urge to spend, refer to your list and find something you can do for free instead.

These are just a few areas where improvements can be made. There are many others, but you have to be willing to cut back. You can't run down your list of expenses over and over again and continue to tell yourself there's nothing that can be cut. Nearly everyone's budget can be trimmed if they're ready to let go of a few luxuries. Like I said in Chapter 1, learning to live more frugally is more about your mind than your money. Once you get into the right frugal mindset, you'll find all kinds of places in your budget where your spending can be cut.

Don't buy anything on the spur of the moment, even if it's on a really great sale. Spur-of-the-moment buying results in unnecessary spending, and impulse buying is not a good idea when you're trying to stick to a budget. Instead, when there's something you want to buy, resist the initial urge. Go home, sleep on it, and see if you still feel as strongly about it 24 hours later. If you still want it and it fits into your budget, do some research and shop around to make sure you're getting the best deal possible. However, many times you'll find that you don't really need or want it as much as you first thought you did.

Stay out of the mall and other stores, including ones online. Lots of people mindlessly shop because they're trying to fill time. Instead, fill your time with things from the list you made of free activities.

Instead of spending time accumulating more, spend your time taking good care of the things you already have. If you spend time taking pride in your possessions, you will be less tempted to just replace them. In addition, taking care of your things will help them last longer, removing the need to replace them frequently. Using what you already have for as long as possible can go a long way toward helping you stay on budget. Here's an example of a way you can take good care of the things you have: Instead of spending your time shopping for a new car, give the one you already have a face lift by vacuuming, washing, and waxing it. Make a list of other ways you can take care of and show pride in the things you already own.

I do believe you have to allow yourself a vice. I guess you could say I subscribe to the "work hard, play hard" philosophy. Life is about balance. But sometimes your vice can get expensive, and although I wouldn't put a person who likes to eat out in the same category as one who has a weakness for luxury cars, any vice can eventually take a toll on your wallet.

The key is moderation. As long as you're staying within your monthly budget, allow yourself a splurge every now and then. But if the urge to splurge is occurring too frequently, you'll need to refer back to your "freebies" list.

If you've cut back on your "I'd rather's" and your budget still isn't balanced, it's time to start looking at your "I have to's." This means examining your mortgage payments and potentially downsizing your home, examining your car payments and potentially getting a cheaper vehicle, or possibly eliminating your summer vacation. Everything is on the table. This may seem severe, but remember: Your budget must be balanced.

Use online banking to implement your budget

After you put your budget in writing and find places to trim it if need be, it's time to put it into action. I'm not going to ask you to only use cash—in fact, quite the opposite. I want you to put technology on your side to help keep your finances in order.

Each month, your income will be deposited into your checking account (and your savings will be deposited into a separate account). First, pay your bills with this money as soon as possible. If you get paid every week, or every other week, you may need to spread the payments out a bit, but pay as much as you can as quickly as you can. The rest is what I'll call a "budget by default." You're free to spend whatever money is left in the account but when it's gone, it's gone.

Check your bank account online, preferably every day but at least every other day, to keep track of how much you're spending and where the money is going. In addition, do not opt in to overdraft protection. If you don't have the money in your account, you want the transaction to be declined rather than pay hefty fees to have it covered.

The Credit Card Accountability Responsibility and Disclosure Act now requires new bank account holders to opt in to overdraft protection for debit card purchases and ATM withdrawals. In the past, most banks provided this service automatically, authorizing your debit card purchase or ATM withdrawal, and then charging a large fee if you didn't have enough money in your account to cover it; now, unless you opt in, those transactions would be declined. The banks try to make it seem like this is a terrible thing. In reality, it's a great thing.

Picture yourself unknowingly close to exceeding your account balance. You swing by the local grocery store to stock up. Your bill is $100, but there's only $90 in your account. The transaction goes through no problem and the bank charges you a $36 overdraft fee. The next morning you swing by the local coffee shop and grab a $2 cup of coffee. Transaction goes through, $36 fee. Your $5 lunch at the fast food joint ends up costing you $41 that day.

Now, let's look at scenario number two. You swing by the local grocery store unaware of how low your account balance has gotten. You spend quite a while filling up your cart and dreaming of the delicious dinner you're going to cook when you get home, but when you swipe your debit card at the check-out counter the transaction is denied. There are several people behind you giving you the evil eye and sighing with impatience. You tell the clerk you're sorry and that he'll have to put your cart full of items back on the shelves. You flee in embarrassment and grumble as you eat a bowl of cereal for dinner while you check your account balance online.

The reality is banks are not doing you any favors by authorizing your transactions when you don't have the money to cover them. Do not opt in to overdraft protection. It may be embarrassing to have your transaction declined, but it's a lot more embarrassing to pay $41 for a burger and fries.

And remember the Credit Card Act rule does not apply to checks, preauthorized electronic payments, and recurring debit card transactions. Banks can continue to pay these items and then charge overdraft fees even without your consent.

What if your categories of spending don't line up exactly with your written budget? That's fine, as long as you're paying all your "I have to's" and having your savings direct deposited into a separate account. After that, your "I'd rathers" are up to you. Your written budget is really just an outline to help you get the big picture on the money you have coming in each month and the money you can afford to have going out, but online banking allows you to have nearly immediate feedback on the details.

Using online banking to implement your budget may seem unconventional compared to other more traditional budgeting and tracking methods, but remember the KISH principle (Keep It Simple, Honey). Budgeting doesn't have to be hard and overly complicated. I want it to be as easy as possible for you to track your spending. This is the age of technology. You're probably used to checking your e-mail and Facebook accounts multiple times a day.

Now all you have to do is get in the habit of checking your online banking each day as well.

Be assertive about your budget

Have you ever found yourself in an awkward money situation? Most people have. Maybe your friends want you and your spouse to go out for a night of fine dining, but you barely have enough money for two Big Macs. Maybe your siblings are all planning a family vacation to the Caribbean, but you don't really want to shell out several thousand dollars for an extravagant trip.

People usually deal with awkward situations, including money situations, in one of three ways: They do whatever they think will cause the least amount of discomfort, they avoid them altogether, or they deal with them directly. Obviously, doing whatever will cause the least amount of discomfort is not a good choice. In the short term, it may seem like a good option, but in the long run, it will only leave you feeling resentful. For instance, you go out to dinner with friends and when the bill arrives, they suggest it be split evenly. However, you're trying to keep a close eye on your budget and know you didn't spend as much on your drinks and meal as the others. For fear of causing an uncomfortable moment, you go along with the suggestion but then feel like you ended up with the short end of the stick. An otherwise-pleasant evening has now been tainted.

If you like to deal with awkward situations by doing your best to avoid them, the scenario might go something like this for you. Your friends ask you to dinner, but you're keeping a close eye on your budget, and because you fear that this might cause a problem when it comes time to pay the bill, you turn down their invitation. For this reason, you begin to repeatedly turn down their invitations. Your friends begin to feel that you're no longer interested in spending time with them, and a divide begins to grow.

By now, it should go without saying that I think the best way to handle these situations is by dealing with them directly. In general, you can handle most of these situations by learning one important phrase, "I have (fill in the blank with a dollar amount) in my budget for that." For example, in relation to the night of fine dining you could say, "I have 40 dollars in my budget for a night out, so I really need to go to a restaurant where I'll be able to stick to that." You can use the same tactic with the family vacation scenario. What if there is no money in your budget for a certain activity? Then say that. If you've committed to only eating at home for a while, let your friends know that eating out just isn't in your budget right now.

This sounds like it should be an easy thing to do but, in reality, it's often more difficult than you'd think. People feel that money matters are private matters. It amazes me that they'll gladly talk about sex or politics, but get all unnerved about discussing their budget.

Instead of addressing the issue head on, many of us engage in what we view to be a socially appropriate dance, in which we respond in the way we feel would be the most well received by others. Certainly, I'm not suggesting that you act rude or crass when someone asks you to split a bill, but I'm definitely suggesting that you make your expectations clear from the beginning. In the case of dinner, ask for separate checks up front. If that's not possible, a statement when the check comes such as "I'm watching my budget closely, so I'll need to calculate what my portion of the bill is" should do the trick.

Remember: When you tell people that you're on a budget, you're not telling them that you're broke but rather that you're smart. Many who don't want to mention budgeting or cutting back are working hard to appear as if they have everything together financially, even when it couldn't be further from the truth. Maybe you can't afford an evening of fine dining. Maybe you can, but you think 50 bucks for one ounce of seafood surrounded by little twigs and dots of sauce is a waste of money. The last time I was at the florist, I told them my budget for a flower arrangement was 35 dollars. Could I have spent more if I had wanted to? Sure, but 35 dollars was what I felt was a reasonable amount.

Keep giving your new message, and you will become comfortable with it. Being direct is a skill that requires practice, but it's a good skill to have. Make your money intentions apparent in a friendly but firm way. And remember: Having a budget doesn't make you poor; it makes you sensible, and that's a message you shouldn't mind making public. Your bank account will thank you for it, too.

Staying on budget during the holidays

Each year holidays become more costly. I think our society has been fooled into thinking that we need to buy a lot of stuff, otherwise known as gifts, for every holiday that comes along. Whether it's Christmas, Chanukah, Valentine's Day, Easter, or birthdays, we frequently find ourselves buying lots of items we can't afford for people who often don't need or even want them. Buying gifts seems to have replaced the true spirit of these occasions.

I stand by the fact that some of the best gifts can't be bought in a store. There are tons of gifts you can give that cost nearly nothing, and I guarantee they'll be much more well-received than those off-the-shelf items the retail world has been trying to convince you to buy. Here are a few ideas:

$ Coupons. No, I don't mean for the grocery store. Remember those coupon books you made as a child? The ones where you wrote, "This coupon is good for...." Maybe you've even received one from your own child. Well, those don't stop being a good idea once you graduate from elementary school. Would your sister rather have another set of towels or a coupon that says you'll babysit her kids on her wedding anniversary? Would your brother rather have another tool set or a coupon that says you'll come help him clean out the garage when spring rolls around?

$ Host a movie night. Find out what movie the recipients want to see and invite them over to watch it. Have popcorn, soda, and a few boxes of candy ready. Consider finishing the evening by playing some cards.

$ Deliver a meal. Whether it's breakfast in bed for your spouse, soup and salad for a friend, or an Italian dinner for a family member, making a meal for someone can be a great gift idea. You'll get to show off your culinary skills, and they'll get a break from the kitchen.

$ Frame a photo. Get an inexpensive frame. Put in it a special photo or collage of photos of you and the recipient together. This is a great way to memorialize good times you've shared.

$ Write a card. I'm talking about a card in which you let the recipient know how special they are and what they've done during the last year that has been important, exceptional, or inspiring. Do you really think your child's teacher wants more knick-knacks to lug home, or would she rather know that you value the difference she's made in your child's education? Does the bus driver really want more stuff, or would he rather hear how much you appreciate him getting your child to school safely each day?

These kinds of gifts aren't cheap; they're thoughtful. Buying something from the store is the easy way out. There are many other things you can do, but you'll have to be a little more creative than just pulling out your wallet.

Holidays provide us with the perfect opportunity to exercise our frugal minds. During these busy times, take a few moments for quiet reflection. Holidays are a time for joy and gratitude. If you have a job, be thankful. If you own a home, consider yourself fortunate. If you have a nice-sized savings account, then you should count your blessings. These are hard economic times for our country. Unemployment is high, stock prices are low, and foreclosures are all too common. You may think these events are the kind that can dampen the excitement of special days and make them less enjoyable. My hope is that the opposite will be true. Maybe they will make us realize that our budgets, whether on a holiday or any other day, are not unlimited. Maybe we'll learn to find more happiness in the things that money can't buy. Next time a holiday rolls around, let your frugal mind take over and tell you that to find joy in your life you don't need to spend lots of money or have, or give, lots of things.

A word about Christmas

No other holiday can make you question the sanity of our society quite like Christmas. Before the Thanksgiving leftovers have even had a chance to cool in the refrigerator, many people have headed out the door to get in line for

Black Friday specials. Some stores open at midnight, while others begin their sales as early as 4 a.m. It's amazing that shoppers, who I'm sure couldn't normally be dragged out of bed at those hours for reasons other than a house fire or hurricane, will eagerly stand in line in the wee hours of the morning to get a Zhu Zhu Pet Hamster or discounted television. Is this really the way we've come to define our priorities?

It's not that I don't appreciate people wanting to get a good deal. I love a great sale just as much as the next person. But if all those people who were standing in line just to save a buck applied that same financial vim and vigor to their lives for the other 364 days of the year, lots of personal income statements would be greatly improved. I guess I just don't believe that's the only reason for the shopping madness.

Everyone knows how hard it is at the holidays to stick to that weight loss plan, and often it's equally as hard to stick to your budget. Just as that eggnog and those Christmas cookies are tempting us to consume extra calories, the constant infusion of holiday commercials and advertisements are tempting us to part with our hard-earned dollars, all in the name of the latest and greatest Christmas gifts. Every time we turn around, we're faced with a barrage of gifts in every price range: less than 20 dollars, less than 50 dollars, less than 100 dollars. Christmas has certainly turned colossally commercial.

Christmas shouldn't be a time for crowded malls, long shopping lists, and free-for-all spending. Nobody wants

a stocking full of debt for Christmas. Don't let your expenditures at the end of the year start you out in the hole
for the next year. Even at the holidays—especially at the
holidays—you must continue to engage your frugal mind
before you start opening up your wallet. Gifts are not really what Christmas is all about.

Has your Christmas list expanded, even though in this
economy your wallet may have shrunk? One of my favorite things to do at Christmas is a white elephant gift exchange. Participants agree to wrap up a useless, used, ugly,
or ridiculous item, preferably from around the house, to
exchange. The point here is to have a few laughs and make
some fun memories, and it costs next to nothing. Don't
blow your budget on Christmas. Christmas shouldn't be
about shopping 'til you drop. It should be a time for re-
membering that some of the best things in life really are
free.

I've always thought that Dr. Seuss did a brilliant job of
presenting us with an anti-commercialism message in his
book *How the Grinch Stole Christmas!* In the words of Dr.
Seuss, "Then the Grinch thought of something he hadn't
before! Maybe Christmas, he thought, doesn't come from
a store. Maybe Christmas...perhaps...means a little bit
more!" You may also remember how, "Every Who down
in Whoville, the tall and the small, was singing, without
any presents at all!" and that, "It came without ribbons! It
came without tags! It came without packages, boxes, or
bags!"[4]

Christmas reminds us that even when the world is insisting that material goods are what matter most, deep down we know it's not true. Try to keep that in mind throughout the year when you feel the urge to overspend or throw your budget out the window. If you can spread that one day's worth of meaning throughout the entire year, your budget can benefit from the true spirit of Christmas the whole year around.

3

Getting Out of Debt

A lesson in debt from Sharon Lechter

In the foreword to this book, Sharon shared her debt lesson (and her son's debt lesson) with us. He had managed to rack up $2,500 in just a few short months. It can be easy to spend today and not worry about tomorrow. But the truth is that debt becomes the seed of stress. It's like a dark cloud hanging over your head that brings with it feelings of instability and even failure. Getting your debt under control is essential for a bright financial future. If you've fallen into this trap, it's time to start digging yourself out.

Paying off debt

Consumer debt is that which is incurred for goods that are consumable or do not appreciate. If you have consumer debt, such as credit cards or payday loans, you need to pay it off. Consumer debt often carries high-interest rates and, unlike mortgage loans, there are no tax benefits associated with it. This means your money is most wisely spent on eliminating these kinds of debts.

Financial gurus have all kinds of advice on how you should determine which debt to pay off first, but in reality there is no one-size-fits-all plan. You need to at least make minimum payments on all of your debts so you don't go into default. After that, some say you should pay off the smallest one first so you feel a sense of accomplishment and motivation to continue down the path of debt elimination. If you're the kind of person that needs to see quick results in order to stay motivated, and paying off a small debt will give you the result you're looking for, then go with that plan.

Some say you should pay off the debt with the highest interest rate first because it'll save the most dollars in interest. If you want to do things based on the numbers and what's going to result in the largest dollar benefit, then go with the highest interest rate first method. Critics will say that if you were worried about the numbers, then you wouldn't have gotten yourself into debt in the first place. There may be some truth to this, but you don't have to be pigeonholed into being a bad money manager for the rest of your life just because you've made some bad decisions. If you've seen the error of your ways and you want to start doing things by the numbers, then by all means do.

Others say you should first pay the minimum amount on your debts and use the remainder to build up your emergency fund, in case you find yourself out of a job and without an income. If you feel like your job situation isn't secure, and it would provide you with a great peace of mind to know that you have cash on hand in case you need it, then make minimum payments on your debt and build up your emergency fund first.

You could also start with the debt that, for whatever reason, bothers you the most, the one that nags at you, the one that keeps you up at night. I call this the "Put Away the Laundry Debt." Putting away the laundry is my absolute least favorite chore to do around the house. I don't mind gathering up the laundry, loading the washer and dryer, or even folding the laundry, but I hate putting it away. I don't know why; it's just something I dread. Stacks of laundry pile up sky high around my house before they finally make their way into drawers and closets. It would be an exaggeration to say that the laundry keeps me up at night, but still, I'd be much better off if I just got it out of the way. I always feel much better once I do.

Do you have a debt about which you feel the same way? Maybe it's one you owe a friend or family member, so it's personal. Perhaps it's a debt that you're particularly mad at yourself for incurring and you just want to see it gone. Or maybe it's the debt about which you've been receiving the most grief from your spouse. If it would be a weight off your shoulders for you to eliminate this debt, work on it first.

There are several debt payoff theories and logical ways in which you can pay down debt. We could spend all day debating the pros and cons of each theory and deliberating about which method is the best, but I say don't worry about the mule, just load the wagon. Which method you pick doesn't matter nearly as much as picking one and starting the process of debt elimination.

You can come up with all kinds of "what if" scenarios. What if I lose my job? What if I can't get anyone to loan me money in the future? What if I don't have the motivation to really make this debt elimination happen? Or you can stop worrying and start doing. Make a list of all your debts; then pick a method or a combination of methods so you can prioritize your debt list and decide the order in which you're going to tackle them. Then buckle down and start loading the wagon or, in this case, unloading the debt wagon.

Student loans

Believe it or not, there's another form of debt that many Americans are encumbered by that actually surpasses the amount owed in credit card debt. This little devil is known as student loan debt. In Chapter 10, I'll discuss what you can do to prevent yourself from falling into the student loan debt trap, but what should you do if you've already acquired this debt? Add it to your debt payoff list, and start eliminating it. If you've already incurred student loans, it's time to tighten your belt (aka. your budget), and start chipping away at that debt. There's no magic wand that can be waved to make it disappear. In fact, even through bankruptcy, it's extremely difficult to discharge student loans. When determining where student loan debt falls on your priority list, keep in mind that, unlike consumer debt, at least some of the interest you pay on your student loan debt is likely deductible on your federal tax return.

The standard student loan plan will typically have a repayment period of 10 years, but that doesn't mean you have to take 10 years to pay it off. You'll want to work on getting student loans paid off as quickly as possible because, like consumer debt, they can have a negative effect on your finances as well as your spirits. It's not fun to be paying for a college experience you're no longer having. In that vein, you should avoid lengthy repayment plans that can extend the term of your loan to anywhere between 12 and 30 years. You don't want to still be paying for college when you should be looking toward retirement.

Even though student loan programs offer deferment or forbearance, which let you temporarily delay or reduce your payments, don't fall back on these options just so you can kick the debt can down the road. Deferment or forbearance should only be considered as an absolute last resort and only when they're the last stop before loan default. If you're truly at that point, *www.studentaid.ed.gov* can give you all the specifics on deferment and forbearance.

Use credit cards wisely

Once you're back on track with your debt, there are several things you can do as far as credit cards go that will help you continue to stay out of trouble:

$ Avoid carrying credit cards in your wallet, and instead only use them when they're the most practical payment method, such as for hotel reservations. If credit cards create way too much temptation for you, then avoid having them around, but remember that if you're looking for the real root of your money issues, your credit card is not the problem. Your lack of a frugal mentality is. There are plenty of people who use credit cards responsibly and yes, there are even people who use their credit cards to their advantage by getting points for things like hotels and cash back. Despite what others might tell you, these people are not fictional creatures like Bigfoot or the abominable snowman. They really do exist, and the only difference between you and them is that they have learned how to mentally master their money. You can, too, not through gimmicks like freezing your card in a glass of water but through embracing frugality.

$ Check your credit card balance online each day. Just like checking your bank account online every day, you should also do the same with your credit card balance. This will help you keep track of how much you're spending and where the money is going.

$ Avoid having multiple credit cards. Multiple cards create unnecessary difficulty in tracking your spending and paying the bills. If you spend a little here and a little there on multiple cards, it may seem that you're not spending much when in reality the number might be large in total. It will also create unnecessary work logging into and checking multiple online accounts as well as having to make payments on multiple cards.

$ Pay in full every month. If you can't pay your card in full every month, you aren't spending based on a balanced budget. Only charge what you have money in the bank to pay for. In addition, you can get socked with hefty interest fees by not paying in full, even if you make partial payments for just a month or two.

$ Pay on time. Again, if you make a late payment, your credit card company is going to hit you with interest and late fees. Don't wait until the last minute to make your payments. Set up e-mail or phone calendar reminders to cue you to pay the bill a few days in advance. If you make a mistake and forget to pay the bill, call the credit card company and ask them to waive the fees. Keep in mind this will pretty much only work once. After that, they'll likely tell you tough luck.

Paying off your debts and staying out of credit card trouble are possible, but remember they have to be part of a plan that centers on embracing a frugal mentality and making a commitment to a balanced budget.

Check and repair your credit report

Your credit report will be reviewed by others when you apply for a mortgage, a car loan, and other forms of credit, as well as when you apply for insurance and even a job, so it's important that you know what's in your report. Your credit report contains identification information such as your name, birth date, Social Security number, and spouse's name. It also includes your account history, such as how much credit you have and whether or not your account payments have been timely, as well as information on any bankruptcies or foreclosures. Banks will use your report to determine whether or not to lend you money and how much they are willing to lend. Usually, the better your credit score is, the better your interest rate will be, so a clean credit report can have a direct impact on your finances. You should also be monitoring your credit report to ensure there isn't any unauthorized credit being issued in your name. Since identity theft is on the rise, vigilance is important.

When was the last time you checked your credit report? Did you know the Fair Credit Reporting Act guarantees you free access to your credit report once every 12 months from Experian, Equifax, and TransUnion, the three national credit reporting companies?

To get a free copy of your credit report, go to *www.annualcreditreport.com*. This is the only source authorized by the Federal Trade Commission. Many other sites advertise free annual credit reports, but in reality they do charge fees or require you to buy other services. These other companies often advertise on TV and through snail mail or e-mail. In fact, a new law now requires other Websites claiming to offer free credit reports to include a message box on their site that lets consumers know they can get a free report at *www.annualcreditreport.com*. The bottom line is, when you start the process of checking your credit report, don't go anywhere else. You'll have the option to request a report from all three companies (Experian, Equifax, and TransUnion) at once or to request them one at a time. I recommend requesting one every four months. That way you can monitor your credit throughout the entire year.

If you find an error in your credit report, notify the credit reporting company in writing. State the item you are disputing, why you are disputing it, and ask that it be corrected. Include copies of any pertinent documents. Then notify the creditor as well. Although the credit reporting company and creditor are responsible for correcting any errors, ultimately your credit report is your responsibility.

If your credit report indicates that you haven't paid your bills on time and have past due accounts or accounts that have been turned over to a collection agency, or if you have credit cards that are maxed out or over the limit, you're going to need to do some credit repair. First, work on bringing any past due accounts current. If need be, call creditors that you have past due accounts with, explain your situation, and see what they can do to work with you. Next, begin bringing any over-the-limit credit cards back under the limit; then, continue to pay down the balances.

If you're having extreme financial difficulties, which may include that you're considering bankruptcy, you should seek the help of a debt counselor so you can receive specific advice on your individual situation. The Association of Independent Consumer Credit Counseling Agencies and the National Foundation for Credit Counseling can give you the names of reputable, non-profit counselors near you that are required to adhere to industry standards. These counselors can provide free or low-cost credit, housing, and bankruptcy counseling, as well as debt management and financial education services.

Once your credit has been damaged, you won't be able to repair it overnight. A big part of credit repair involves a waiting game, allowing enough time to pass that blemishes drop off your report. In the meantime, be sure you've learned your lesson and embraced a new frugal mentality so you don't find yourself in the exact same position over and over again.

4

Save, Save, and Save Some More

A lesson in savings from my golf pro

After I turned 30 I decided it was time I broadened my horizons, tried things I'd never tried before, did things I saw other women over 30 were doing. First, I decided to take up tennis. I bought a racquet and one of those cute tennis skirts, and headed on over to the court for women's night. There were several other beginners there. We chatted, had a few drinks, and missed at least every other ball that came our way. Overall, though, the experience was a pleasant one. I've never been athletically inclined. Really, the only sport I'd be qualified to coach, even for little league, is cheerleading. And I know you're probably thinking it's debatable that cheerleading can even be called a sport. But I left that evening feeling good that at least I hadn't made a total fool out of myself.

I attended a few more clinics, bought another skirt (on clearance, of course), and even signed up for a pink ribbon tennis tournament to raise money for breast cancer research. I was diggin' this tennis thing. I clearly belonged in the beginner league, but I wasn't terrible, and I could play a game of doubles without being a complete embarrassment to my partner.

My branching out experience was so enjoyable, that I decided I should add another sport to my repertoire. There was a company golf tournament coming up, so I convinced two of my coworkers and a friend that we should enter a women's team. I told them how much fun we would have, how no one would notice or care if we stunk, and how good the free food would be. In what was clearly a moment of weakness combined with delusion (one of my coworkers had never hit a golf ball before in her life and the other played very infrequently), they agreed. I assured them we'd be fine. My friend was very good at golf, and this was a captain's choice tournament. We could just play her ball every time if we needed to.

Nonetheless, because I had never hit a golf ball before either, I decided I should take some lessons. I called the local driving range and made an appointment to meet with the golf pro. He convinced me to make a commitment to four lessons, which seemed reasonable considering I was starting from square one.

The first lesson involved a lot of holding the club, or "working on my grip," as the pro called it. He gave me a nine iron, or maybe it was a seven, and after he showed me how to wrap my hands around it he took me out to practice hitting the ball, something that proved to be much harder than it sounded. I can't tell you how many times I swung and completely missed, but if I had a nickel for every time it happened, I could've more than paid for the lessons. When I did manage to actually hit the ball, it usually went all of about 5 yards.

The pro seemed unfazed by this—I'm assuming he's tutored many a golf moron in his day—but I was frustrated. I did quite a bit of sighing and eye rolling, and commented frequently on my lack of athletic prowess. But at the end of the hour, I scheduled my second lesson for a few days later.

The next session went pretty much like the first, except we spent more time working on my swing. "Relax," he told me, followed by a lot of talk about loosening my grip and following through. I hit a few more balls than I did before, but I really didn't notice any significant improvement. It wasn't the pro's fault. He was nice and patient, and he had an impressive resume, but I was in no way a natural. I watched all the other golfers around me. They made it look so easy. Their club made that nice "whack" sound as it connected with the ball and made it fly across the green. My club made a "swish" as it sliced through nothing but air. More sighing, eye rolling, and self-degradation ensued on my part, and yet I scheduled the next session.

Half-way through the third lesson, I had turned noticeably offish and sarcastic about the whole thing. I'm sure by this time the pro was probably feeling like he had an unsatisfied customer on his hands. Finally he turned to me and said, "You don't seem to be enjoying this at all. The people I teach usually like golf and think it's fun. What would make you like this more?" I looked him square in the eye and said, "I would like this more if I was better at it." As soon as the words came out of my mouth I started to laugh. "I really stink at this," I said.

I took the fourth lesson, but unfortunately by the time it was over I couldn't say the same thing about golf that I had about tennis. I was terrible, and I was a complete embarrassment to the women's team at the company tournament. Luckily, I was good at driving the cart and keeping the beer cold, so I wasn't a complete waste.

More importantly, the pro had inadvertently taught me something about saving. No one would argue that saving is a bad thing. How could it not be fun to have a big stash of money? But clearly a lot of people don't enjoy saving, maybe because they're not good at it yet. Simply put, saving means not spending. If you're not spending money, you're saving it, and many people aren't good at not spending.

I've continued to play golf. The pro assured me that the way you get good at hitting a golf ball is by swinging at it over, and over, and over. Just like golf, saving takes practice. If you do it regularly and routinely, you will get good at it. And when you get good at it, you'll start to enjoy it.

The savings challenge: 20 percent

Saving is about delayed gratification. It's about forgoing some of the things that might be nice to have now in order to ensure that you have enough for a lifetime. For many people, saving doesn't come naturally. It takes discipline, commitment, and some good old-fashioned willpower.

Savings is a crucial part of any financial plan and most Americans don't have enough of it. The personal savings rate for the second quarter of 2012 was 4 percent.[1] If you are one of those people who are currently saving nothing, then 4 percent would be a step in the right direction. Anything would be a step in the right direction, but 4 percent is not enough for the long run.

I'm going to challenge you to save—a lot. Twenty percent of your income is the number I have in mind, and I realize to some of you that may seem huge. After all, you have many things you need to pay for, but just think of all the things you need to save for. You may be saving for a home or for making improvements to your home. If you have dependent children, there's college tuition. And don't forget about retirement. The list of tomorrow's needs is just as long as that of today.

The three-phase savings plan

Saving does require a certain amount of willpower. You can't set up a savings account and then dip into it every time you want a new outfit or an evening out with friends. Saving often requires adjusting your budget and your spending. It means that you might have to go without some of the things you want to establish the savings that you need.

Once you are consumer debt free or in conjunction with your debt payoff, you need to establish, or perhaps enhance, your emergency fund. Do you have at least $1,000 in a savings account? If your answer is no, you should make it a priority to stash away enough to have a minimum $1,000 dollar safety net. If you already have that much saved, you've made it over the first hurdle. Now, you need to work on setting aside enough to cover six months worth of living expenses in case you lose your job, become ill, or find yourself in some other emergency situation. Don't keep your emergency fund at your regular bank. It will be too easy and too tempting to pull money out. Put your emergency fund in the bank across town where it's not as easily accessible, because this account is only for true emergencies.

When your emergency fund is established, you can start working on your other savings goals. To ensure that your bank account becomes a savings success story, you need a good savings plan. My savings plan has three phases:

1. The Piggy Bank Phase.
2. The Paying Yourself First Phase.
3. The Goal Phase, Short-Term and Long-Term.

The Piggy Bank Phase

If your finances have gotten so out of control that you're feeling overwhelmed by the thought of saving 20 percent, then start small. You won't be doing yourself any favors by setting unrealistic goals and not seeing any progress. Small changes can add up and give you a way to find those extra dollars to put into savings. When you're starting small, where you put the money is not important. Just start saving something. Put it in a piggy bank or even a jar for ease of deposit.

Find small ways where you can cut spending and have dollars to put in your pig. I'm not going to tell you to avoid Starbucks, skip the restaurant meals, and equip all your light fixtures with compact fluorescent light bulbs, although all of those things would likely save you money. What I want you to do is pick one thing per day that you're going to do in order to save.

Albert Einstein is attributed with the quote "Insanity: doing the same thing over and over again and expecting different results." If you haven't been able to save in the past or if your savings isn't at the level it should be, you need to do something different, something that will add to your savings each day. It's your choice, but you must do one thing per day, as small consistent changes will add up.

Do the math

$ Monday—Skip the tall latte and brew your own coffee instead. Money in your piggy bank: $3.

$ Tuesday—Bring your lunch from home instead of eating fast food. Money in your piggy bank: $5.

$ Wednesday—Cook dinner at home instead of picking up a pizza after work. Money in your piggy bank: $10.

$ Thursday—Rent a DVD from Red Box instead of ordering pay-per-view. Money in your piggy bank: $4.

$ Friday—Have one less beer at happy hour. Money in your piggy bank: $4.

$ Saturday—Buy a generic product instead of name brand. Money in your piggy bank: $3.

$ Sunday—Purchase a shirt on clearance instead of regular price. Money in your piggy bank: $10.

$ Total dollars in your piggy bank for the week: $39.

Saving each day is good training for your frugal mind. Some days you'll do smaller things to save and some days you'll do larger things, but finding one way to save each day serves two purposes. First, it puts dollars in the bank and, as you see those dollars adding up, you'll be motivated to continue. Second, it keeps saving at the forefront of your mind. It makes you more aware of the ways in which you're spending your money and the fact that there are many opportunities to reduce that spending.

Finding one way to save every day may sound like a lot of work, but if you start continually looking for those opportunities, soon it will become second nature. Get your family members involved in coming up with savings ideas or team up with friends. Share and swap tips, and provide encouragement to each other. Make it a point to congratulate yourself each week that you put dollars in the piggy bank, but don't do it by spending money. Instead, congratulate yourself with some "me time." Take an hour for yourself and read a book, watch your favorite TV show, or do some gardening. Remember: Small changes and small amounts will eventually add up to big savings as your frugal side takes over.

The Paying Yourself First Phase

Once you've seen that you can find ways to save, you won't want to continue to sock your money away in a piggy bank. For phase two, a savings account will be the best place for your money. Now that you're ready for the next phase of your savings plan, you'll want to continue to save on a regular basis and work on increasing the amount you save. The easiest way to do this is by having the money taken directly out of your paycheck and automatically deposited into your savings account. This is called paying yourself first. Paying yourself first goes along with the "out of sight, out of mind" principle. If you never see the money, you will be less likely to miss it and less likely to blow it on a weekend shopping spree.

If you need to, start with 5 percent and re-evaluate your savings amount every three months. Work toward increasing the amount by 2–3 percent at a time, with an ultimate goal of reaching 20 percent. You'll still be looking for ways to save each day, but now that daily savings will be in addition to the amount that you've automatically had deducted from your paycheck.

When you do your three-month review, ask yourself what you did well. Resolve to continue those accomplishments and take them to the next level. Then take a look at what you didn't do well and need to work on. Analyze why things went wrong and come up with a new strategy to address them in the future.

Consider whether you want to have one savings account that includes both your emergency fund and additional savings, or whether you want to have two separate accounts. If you go with two separate accounts, make sure you have your second savings account deposited somewhere other than your regular bank, just like your emergency fund. If you have it deposited at your regular bank, it will be too easy and too tempting to make a few little or big withdrawals here and there. If you have to drive to the other side of town to a bank you wouldn't normally go to, you'll think twice before making the trip. This might sound like the freezing your credit card gimmick, and it's true that, if you've embraced a frugal mentality, then it won't matter which bank you keep your savings at. However, the point is to make a clear distinction between your spending money and your savings.

The Goal Phase, Short-Term and Long-Term

Saving is about making a commitment to your future. This includes saving for expenses you know are coming. Get ahead of the game by planning and saving for these upcoming expenses. Are you going on vacation? Are you going to need a new vehicle soon? Is your washing machine nearing the end of its useful life? Don't be caught without the money to pay cash for these kinds of things. These are not emergencies. Let me repeat that: If you can plan for an event, it is not an emergency. You have to make it a short-term goal to budget and save for these things. Vacations, a new or preferably used car, and appliances should consume a small amount of your savings because these are non-investment items. Make savings for them part of your regular budget.

What will continue to motivate you to save for the long term? As you see the money piling up, you'll feel a sense of independence. When you have to rely on credit cards and bank loans, you are at the mercy of the credit card companies and the banks. Savings is power. Saving is not about restriction, but about the freedom to do what you want and have the things you want.

What are your long-term savings goals? Here are some common things people want to save for:

$ Retirement. This usually tops the list of long-term goals, although it may not seem too exciting at this point in your life. But what about early retirement or saving to make sure you have a really nice retirement that includes something like a condo on the golf course? Those are goals you might be able to get more excited about.

$ Home-related savings. Maybe you're saving for a down payment on your first home or upgrades and repairs on your current home. Perhaps you're saving for a second home at the beach, at the lake, or in the mountains.

$ Investment property. Would you like to own a house, townhouse, or condo for rental purposes?

$ Owning your own business.

$ College for your children. More about this in Chapter 9.

Set some specific long-term goals and put them in writing. There are so many things to save for that sometimes it can feel overwhelming. I don't want you to save everything for tomorrow and not enjoy today. I'd rather you look for ways to do both. You're going to have to be the judge of what you save for and what you spend on. Although you want to have savings goals, you don't have to decide which goal every dollar is going to go toward right now. It's important to have goals so that you'll continue to stay motivated, but accumulating the dollars is the most important part. And remember: Frugal people hate to tap into their savings. They do it only when absolutely necessary, to the smallest extent possible, and the majority of their savings will go toward things that are good investments.

Other savings opportunities

Throughout your life, there will be big money events that will allow you to quickly add large amounts to your savings account. When these big money events take place, the key is to apply the 80/20 rule in reverse. Instead of spending 80 percent and saving 20 percent, you're going to spend 20 percent and save 80 percent. Here are some examples of big money events:

$ Bonuses. Always bank 80 percent of any bonuses you get at work. If you're trying to pay off debt or beef up your savings account, you should save 80 percent of any raises you get as well. Your spending does not need to increase by the same amount that your earnings increase. I realize it's unlikely that you'll keep the exact same standard of living as your income goes up, but limit your additional spending to 20 percent and put the difference into savings.

$ Tax refunds. Brace yourself; the advice I'm about to give defies all conventional wisdom on this topic. Claim zero on your W-4 to have your employer deduct the maximum tax withholdings from your paycheck. Financial experts will typically tell you that overpaying your taxes each month is like giving the government an interest-free loan. Instead, you should be investing that money and earning a return. But let's face it; most people aren't disciplined enough to actually do that. The extra money will just get lost in the shuffle, and there won't be anything to show for it at the end of the year. Claiming zero is like a forced savings, except your account isn't sitting at the local bank, so there's no way you can get your hands on it. And there's something motivational about receiving a lump sum on your tax return. Hopefully, along with a nice chunk of change will come the realization that you don't want to waste it.

$ The sale of a home. If you made a smart home purchase (more about that in Chapter 6), you should have some equity to cash out when you sell it. Don't use this money to buy a house twice the size of the one you sold. Instead, save it.

$ An inheritance. I'm not suggesting that your savings plan should depend on Great Aunt Agnes moving on to that big ranch in the sky, but if you come into an inheritance, don't blow it; save it.

$ Gifts. Graduations and weddings are two examples of times in your life when you might receive large monetary gifts. If you have wealthy family members, you may also receive large amounts for Christmas and birthdays. Don't be fooled into thinking that you owe it to the gift giver to spend the money on something nice. You owe it to yourself to save that money. A large sum of money coming your way may seem like a windfall and cause for a spending celebration. But it's far better to use that money to further your financial security.

5

Creating an Investment Plan That Works for You

A lesson in investing from my two alpacas

My husband and I had been living in a subdivision for nearly two years when our dream home came on the market. We made an offer immediately on the 100-year-old farmhouse on three acres, with lots of large trees and a pond. A month later, we packed up, left suburbia behind, and moved four blocks down the road to the country. When you live in rural southwest Virginia, there's not a big difference between the two.

The front acre of our new home was fenced in to create a pasture of a decent size. Every time I looked at it, I felt like it seemed empty without any animals roaming around. It was practically calling out for some sort of livestock, so I began my search for the perfect animal to put on our land.

First, we considered a horse. They're beautiful to look at and fun to ride. They're also expensive and high maintenance and, to tell you the truth, I think they're kind of big and scary. So we ruled out a horse. Then we considered goats. Goats are friendly and make good pets, but they're destructive. They're excellent escape artists, and they eat everything in sight. Our fence matched our house in that it too looked to be 100 years old, and I was sure it stood no chance against the likes of a few goats. I pictured them easily getting out and munching on my landscaping. So we ruled out goats as well. We thought about pigs, but decided they were too smelly, and sheep, but my husband had raised those growing up and was sick of them.

One evening we were discussing our dilemma with a friend, and she suggested that we look into getting alpacas. I was sure she was joking when she said it, but she convinced me that she was serious and that her suggestion deserved consideration. She told me that alpacas were low maintenance, non-destructive, not smelly, and unique—pretty much everything we'd been looking for.

I thought alpacas seemed too exotic, not like the typical farm animals I had been thinking of, but I looked online and found a local alpaca farm, so my husband and I paid them a visit. The alpacas were actually very cute and fluffy. They were a good size, not too big and not too small. I also discovered that they only have bottom teeth, so they can't bite you, and they have pads on their feet, not hard hooves. I was starting to think that alpacas really were the perfect animal for me. Then I discovered the price. These alpacas had a price tag of thousands of dollars. They were expensive because they were all being sold for breeding purposes. I quickly discovered that people don't really have alpacas as farm animals. After all, you don't use them for their milk or meat. People have alpacas as an investment.

I'm the kind of person who's continually on the lookout for an investment. I also have to say that I rarely end up making those investments. My risk tolerance is quite low. But I'm always open to hearing the pitch, and I learned right away that the alpaca breeders wanted to give me the pitch. They wanted to sell me females to be bred and males to do the siring, all so I could have more little baby alpacas, called "crias," to sell. The problem with alpacas is that there's really no market for them other than to sell them to other people just so they can turn around and breed them to sell to other people. Sure they have very choice fleece, or "fiber," as it's called, but there's really no mass market for alpaca fiber like there is for wool.

However, I did find the alpaca to be the ideal animal for my purposes. I discovered that they require little care, are so skittish that they would never dream of trying to escape from my less-than-fortress-like fence, and even poop in a pile. Yes, you read that right. Instead of creating a pasture full of land mines, alpacas are a very tidy sort.

Still, I decided that the alpaca investment was not for me for a few reasons. First, I certainly wasn't educated enough about the investment to be putting up that kind of money. At that point, my knowledge of the animal was limited to having watched the Ilovealpacas.com commercial a few times. I'd hardly say that made me a qualified investor. Second, the potential for return just wasn't there. It's easy to get swept away when someone is giving you their sales pitch, but after the excitement wears off, you have to decide whether or not the dollars and cents of the deal really do add up. Third, I have to be honest: I'm not really a big animal person, so I didn't think starting up an alpaca breeding operation would be my forte.

I did think alpacas were cool though, so I found a large breeder that was selling her less-desirable animals cheaply. I picked up two for 400 bucks and figured it was a reasonable price to pay for my interesting lawn ornaments. And don't worry, I won't be doing any breeding. They're both males.

When it comes to investing you have to be educated and assertive. There are plenty of people out there that will try to sell you anything, from emus and alpacas to options contracts and index funds. You have to learn how to separate the wheat from the chaff, so to speak. There's nothing wrong with listening to the pitch. In fact, you can learn a lot by investigating a variety of investment choices, but always be prepared to make your own decisions about what's right for you and what isn't.

The importance of financial education

Being financially literate means having the knowledge that will enable you to effectively manage your finances, make wise decisions, and attain your goals. It means being informed so you can be in control of your financial future and make the best decisions for you and your family. Like so many other things in life, a big part of being financially successful is education. According to a 2012 survey conducted for the National Foundation for Credit Counseling by Harris Interactive, 42 percent of adults surveyed gave themselves a grade of C, D, or F on their knowledge of personal finance.[1]

Investing is a key area of personal finance that requires financial literacy. When it comes to investing, education can make the difference between a solid plan and wishful thinking. You don't have to be an investing genius to be financially literate, but if you're going to make investments, you do have to take the time to learn about them. Even if you're only planning to invest in mutual funds via a 401(k) plan or IRA, you have to evaluate your options thoroughly and become informed of all the choices. If you are asking yourself right now, "What's a mutual fund? What's a 401(k)?" then you have some serious work to do. Unlike past generations who worked for the same company until they retired and then relied on that company to provide them with a nice pension, the workers of today will have to rely on their own investments for continued income.

Even if you already have money in the market, you need to go through the research process if you haven't done so in the past. Visit the Websites of some of the large brokerage firms, such as Fidelity, Charles Schwab, or whatever firm you have or are considering having manage your investments, and request their information be mailed to you. Although this material may not be what you had in mind for nighttime reading, it will give you lots of details about your investment options.

Explore the options your employer offers with regard to financial education. Even if you can't count on them for a pension, you may be able to rely on them for some education programs. In addition, consider attending an investment seminar; read articles and watch news programs about investing. When you have knowledge, you are in control of your own financial destiny.

Put the "I" back in investing

You shouldn't put your money into anything you don't really understand. If someone came to you and wanted you to buy a piece of real estate in another country, you would be skeptical. You would ask tons of questions. Even though you know, generally speaking, what a house is, you would be very cautious about forking over your hard-earned money until you made yourself comfortable with the details of the transaction. The stock market is no different. For many people, it's also foreign territory. Don't invest until you understand what you're investing in.

You may be thinking that the stock market is too complicated for you. That's why you have a broker or financial advisor, and I'm not against that. But having a broker or advisor is no substitute for gaining your own knowledge, because nobody cares about your money as much as you do.

Think about it. Would you walk onto a car lot and say to the salesperson, "I don't know much about cars, but you just tell me what you think I should get and I'll write out the check"? No, you wouldn't. You would do some online or magazine research. You'd study things such as safety features and miles per gallon, and shop around for the best deal.

If you had a serious illness and went to the doctor, he or she would give you a treatment plan. Even if you trusted your doctor, you'd probably get a second opinion. You'd study online, and glean information from friends and family members. Be sure you're doing the same thing when it comes to your investments. Ask many questions, and be aware that what you are reading and hearing is a sales pitch aimed at selling you investment products. Remember: Never ask a barber if he thinks you need a haircut. He'll tell you yes every time.

There are high-quality financial advisors that can provide you with good investment information and advice, but you still need to be an active participant in the process. Do your research; look into things yourself, and have financial discussions with family, friends, and other people who can provide you with additional insight. Even if you trust your advisor, you should always be open to other opinions. Most importantly, think for yourself.

In addition, don't be pressured into anything that doesn't feel right to you. No one can guarantee that you'll make a profit on your investments. In fact, most investments open you up to the potential for loss. That's why it's important that if you don't feel comfortable with a particular investment, steer clear of it. Stick to safer investments such as bonds or even CDs or savings accounts. I know most people will tell you that if you put your money into a CD or savings account, the rate of return these investments offer doesn't even allow you to keep up with inflation. Though mathematically this might be true, how many people have you ever known to reach their golden years and say, "Gosh, I wish I had less money in these CDs," or "Golly, I wish my savings account had a smaller balance." Is it possible that someday you'll look back and say, "Boy, I really wish I'd bought that stock," or "Wow, if I had only bought that condo, it's worth so much more now." But that's just a lot of coulda, woulda, shoulda. Hindsight is always 20/20, but when it comes to investing, you can only act in the here and now, making the best decisions possible with the information currently available.

You may have heard that the quickest way to double your money is to fold it over and put it back in your pocket. I believe there's a good bit of truth to that. Don't be greedy, and don't fool yourself into thinking that there are investments out there that are low risk and high return. If an investment seems too good to be true, it probably is. If someone offers you this kind of opportunity, they're likely offering you the opportunity to lose your shirt. Investments with a greater potential for return will always come with a greater potential for risk. There is a trade-off between peace of mind and potential for profit.

Assess your risk tolerance and make your investments accordingly. Remember: It's your money. You have the ultimate responsibility for it. Only make investment decisions that you are truly comfortable with.

401(k)s and IRAs

For many people, running a retirement calculator is kind of like shaking a magic eight ball that's only been programmed with one answer: Outlook Not So Good. Should you save for retirement? Absolutely. Is the number 33 percent of your income? Maybe. But even if it was, is there any chance you'd start saving that much just for retirement? My point is this: Don't spend all of today trying to anticipate tomorrow. Don't get so hung up on the huge amount the calculator tells you should be saved each month that you begin to feel it's hopeless that you'll ever be able to retire. Just start contributing what you can to a retirement savings account or continue to stick with it if you've already started, and make it a goal to increase the amount you contribute gradually, once every six months or once every year.

A 401(k) is a retirement savings account that is funded by your contributions and matching contributions from your employer. The amount your employer will match is considered an employee benefit and will vary from company to company. One of the main benefits of a 401(k) is that your contributions are deducted from your paycheck pre-tax. The account then grows tax free until you start making withdrawals.

You should start investing in a 401(k) as soon as you get your first job with an employer that offers the plan. The earlier you start contributing, the longer you'll have for your money to accumulate and grow. When it comes to retirement savings, you always want to put time on your side. A 401(k) also allows you to take responsibility for your own retirement destiny. Who knows what will happen with Social Security? With consistent payroll deductions, you can start saving for your own retirement on a regular basis.

Another benefit of the 401(k) is the match that the employer contributes on top of your personal contributions. The fact that your employer is giving you free money makes the 401(k) a very attractive retirement savings vehicle. Be sure to take full advantage of this free money. At a minimum, you should invest an amount that will maximize the employer match. For example, if your employer will match 100 percent of the first 3 percent you contribute and 50 percent of the next 3 percent you contribute, then you should put in at least 6 percent to your 401(k) to take full advantage of the employer match.

The amount you choose to contribute beyond what will be matched is up to you. It will depend on where retirement fits into your savings priorities and how much of your savings you want tied up in a 401(k) account, because you shouldn't be tapping into it until your later years. Once you put funds into the account, you will not be able to withdraw them without a minimum penalty of 10 percent, unless you are eligible to make withdrawals either because you have reached the minimum age of 59 and a half or be-cause you've proven that you have certain hardships. In ad-dition, the amount you withdraw will then become taxable as well. Generally, once you put the money in the 401(k) account, you'll want to leave it there until you reach the minimum age for penalty-free withdrawal.

Within your 401(k) plan, you will be able to choose how you want your money invested. The portfolio you choose will depend on how long you have until retire-ment and what your personal risk tolerance is. If you have a long time until retirement, most advisors will recom-mend higher-risk investments that are also likely to bring a higher return over time. Whether or not you are com-fortable with a higher-risk portfolio will depend on your personal risk tolerance. If you tend to shy away from risk, consider a more diversified portfolio that contains a mix of low and high risk investments. If the stock market crash in 2008 has made you leery, there's also nothing wrong with a mostly low-risk portfolio. Remember: It's your money. You have to do what feels right to you. Consider also that the 403(b) account is for university, civil government, and not-for-profit employees, and has the same characteristics and benefits of the 401(k).

An IRA is an Individual Retirement Account. If you don't work for an employer that offers a 401(k), you might want to consider an IRA. This type of retirement savings account is funded by your contributions, but un-like the 401(k), there are no matching contributions. Like the 401(k), the IRA has tax benefits. Also, similar to the 401(k), you won't want to make withdrawals until you reach the age of 59 and a half. There are two types of IRAs available that you'll want to consider depending on your individual needs.

The first is a traditional IRA. With the traditional IRA, the amount you deposit in the account will be exempt from income tax. At the time of withdrawal, the funds will then be taxable. With the second IRA, the Roth IRA, there are no tax benefits on the funds you contribute, but after you reach 59 and a half the funds you withdraw are not taxable. As you can see, the traditional IRA is better if you anticipate being in a lower tax bracket when you retire and the Roth IRA is better if you anticipate being in a higher tax bracket when you retire.

Retirement savings accounts are subject to many unknowns, in addition to the question of what tax bracket you'll be in when you retire; there are no guarantees on rate of return either. Some people love retirement savings accounts and invest every extra dollar they have in them. Even if you don't feel quite that strongly about these kinds of accounts, you should definitely be saving something for retirement. Set some realistic savings goals for yourself and you'll be on your way to a more secure retirement.

Employee Stock Purchase Plans and stock trading accounts

An Employee Stock Purchase Plan (ESPP) is a benefit that allows employees to purchase stock in the corporation they work for at a discount. This discount varies, but can be as much as 15 percent. Instead of purchasing a certain number of shares, employees decide what percentage of their paycheck they want to put toward the plan. The maximum amount employees can elect to contribute is usually 10 percent. Those dollars are then deducted from their paycheck and used to buy shares of stock at the discounted price. The number of dollars contributed will determine how many shares can be purchased.

Employers offer this benefit so that employees can share in the success of the company and to give employees a vested interest in seeing the company succeed. If your employer has an ESPP, you should seriously consider participating. Decide what percentage of your budgeted savings you want to go toward the ESPP, and let your employer know so they can begin deducting that amount from your paycheck. Most plans will allow you to increase or decrease this amount throughout the year.

ESPPs offer a good way to boost your savings and build wealth. Instead of waiting years to watch your money grow, the discounted price ESPPs offer adds an instant growth factor to your investment. Although on paper you will have an immediate profit upon the purchase of your shares, no income is reported until you sell the stock and actually realize that profit. If you choose to turn around and sell the shares right away, the gain will be taxed at your ordinary income tax rates. Ordinary income tax rates apply to short-term capital gains or gains on assets held for one year or less. However, if you hang on to the shares for more than a year, you have the potential to further maximize your profits through additional stock price growth and the ability to take advantage of the lower long-term capital gains tax rate. If you choose to invest in an ESPP, you'll have to decide if you're going to take the money and run, or stay in the game for a while and try to maximize your gains.

ESPPs are typically easy to understand and convenient to set up, making them an ideal investment to add to your portfolio. Plans do vary from company to company, so be sure to get a copy of the written material that gives all the details of your employer's plan and learn the specifics of how your plan works.

ESPPs are an easy way to get started in the stock market, but if your employer doesn't offer one of these plans or if you want to invest in more than just your company's stock, you may want to consider setting up your own trading account with a discount online brokerage company so you can buy and sell stocks yourself. Because of Internet technology, it's possible for anyone who wants to invest in the stock market to make his or her own trades. Scottrade, OptionsHouse, and TradeKing are examples of discount online brokerage firms. Obviously, the stocks you purchase through your own account won't come at an employer discount, but a trading account that you control will provide you the opportunity to get discounts on the trading fees and commissions you'd be charged if you had a full-service broker buying and selling stocks for you.

A cash account is the most basic kind of brokerage account and the one you'll want to start with. Beginning balances required to open an account are typically low, and when you're ready to begin making real trades, you can fund your account by check, electronic transfer, or cashing in a stock certificate you already have. You should make sure that the money you deposit is going to sit in an FDIC-insured account, preferably an interest-bearing one, when it's not being invested in stocks. When you place a buy order, your money will be taken from your insured account to purchase the stock, and when you sell a stock, the proceeds will go back into your insured account.

Most trading platforms (the program you'll be using to do your buying and selling) have become very user-friendly. What making your own trades does require, though, besides a fast Internet connection, is that you learn some simple vocabulary and mechanics of buying and selling stocks, and then doing research on which stocks you want to buy. Before you make real trades in your account, it would be wise to take a workshop, either online or in person, or at minimum to go through the tutorial that your trading company offers. Most of these companies also offer a paper trading system that simulates trading live in the stock market and allows you to practice making trades without using real money.

Managing your own trading account may seem overwhelming at first, but putting some time into learning how to trade stocks can be well worth it, as you are in control of your own money, rather than handing all the decisions over to someone else.

Real estate

Some people will find investing in real estate more comfortable than the stock market because they've already gone through the process of purchasing a home and are therefore familiar with the details of a real estate transaction. Just like purchasing a home, investing in real estate will require some preparation on your part. You'll need to do some investment analysis before you make your purchase.

I recommend buying a property for renting rather than flipping. Flipping is a short-term investment that is typically very labor intensive and requires more available cash. Types of properties you should think about for rentals are condos, townhouses, and houses. For your first real estate investment, it would be wise to consider these kinds of residential properties rather than commercial properties or larger ones such as apartment complexes. Zoning in on a specific type of property or location that you're interested in will help refine your search.

In order to find the best real estate investment possible, having an experienced and trustworthy real estate professional on your side is essential. Real estate agents find out about properties as soon as they hit the market and often even beforehand. This kind of timely information is very valuable in the real estate world. If you have a real estate agent you can trust, you can also ask his or her personal opinion about whether or not a particular property would be a good investment. In addition, a real estate professional can advise you on all aspects of the purchase transaction.

To purchase an investment property you're going to need a down payment, typically 20 percent. There are many real estate investment programs that will try to convince you that you can own half your town with no money down. I'm sure you've seen some of these gimmicks on late-night TV. If you're looking to launch a successful real estate investment career, you'll want to look into a variety of financing options. However, for a smaller, "on-the-side" real estate investment, you'll want to have 20 percent saved. If you don't have the money for the down payment, you have no business making the investment in the first place. You'll also need a good, steady income and good credit in order to make this kind of investment. Having an experienced and trustworthy mortgage broker on your side is also essential.

If you're interested in purchasing an investment property, you'll need to do some market research and find one where you can at least break even. This means that the rent coming in is at least enough to cover the mortgage payment, taxes, insurance, homeowner's dues, utilities, maintenance and repairs, and any other costs associated with the rental. With a breakeven property, you'll be looking to make your money from the appreciation, or increase in value, of the property over time. However, a property that generates positive cash flow, especially significant positive cash flow, is ideal. This means the rent coming in is more than enough to cover all of the expenses, and you'll have additional cash left over each month. Depending on the real estate market in your area, properties that generate significant positive cash flow can be difficult to find.

If you're going to start your search from scratch, find out what prices properties are selling for, what level rent they generally bring in, and whether or not they're continuously occupied. You'll also need to factor maintenance and repair costs into your analysis. Be sure you're not cutting things too close and can weather a few months with the property unoccupied.

Another excellent way to get started in the real estate investment world is by hanging on to, rather than selling, a property that you currently own but for whatever reason have outgrown. If, for example, you bought a townhouse when you got your first job but are now ready to move into a single family home, keep the townhouse rather than selling it, and rent it out. If your credit and cash flow will allow it, this can be the easiest and most painless way to acquire an investment property, because you don't have to go through all the usual trouble of acquiring a property; you already own it.

6

How to Make Those Large Purchases Work

A lesson in home buying from my days at the lake

My husband had always wanted to live at the lake. I didn't feel particularly drawn to having a home on the water, but because there wasn't any other area that I did feel particularly drawn to, we decided that was where we would focus our search for our first home together. We contacted a real estate agent and began looking for the perfect home. In my mind, the perfect home had a nice yard, an appealing exterior, and an attractive, spacious interior.

I realized right away that there were very few homes at the lake in our price range and only one in the closer-to-town location that we wanted to be in, so we made an appointment with our agent to see the home. I was less than impressed as the house came into view. The exterior was constructed of cedar siding that looked like it hadn't been stained in several years. The walkway to the front door was just some thrown-down gravel and beside it was a lovely stone retaining wall that was only half-finished.

Upon entering the home, I quickly discovered that the interior left much to be desired as well. It had no air conditioning, the upstairs bathroom was extremely outdated, and the tacky wallpaper in the bedrooms was peeling off the walls. I wanted to check the house off the list immediately, but my husband really liked it. Despite its flaws, the home sat on a very nice piece of waterfront property with two docks in a quiet cove. The water view from the master bedroom window was just lovely, and although it had a very small yard, two expansive decks were connected to both the upper and lower levels of the house. My husband insisted that these things outweighed the home's faults, and although I was still largely unconvinced, we made an offer.

It was winter, not a booming season for lake home sales, and the house had been on the market for several months and was sitting empty. The price on it had been recently reduced to $159,000. We made an offer of $150,000, $9,000 below the asking price, which we assessed had already been lowered to a very reasonable level in an attempt to get it sold. The owner accepted it without a counteroffer and before I knew it, we had bought ourselves a home at the lake. In hindsight, we should have negotiated a bit harder and made a lower initial offer, but at that time, neither of us had much experience making large purchases. Even so, we got the home for a great price.

We began making improvements immediately and started with the ones that were most pressing. All the wallpaper came down, every room was painted, and the cedar siding and decking were stained. During the next four years, we continued to update things, including adding a heat pump, remodeling the bathroom, finishing the sidewalk and retaining wall, and several other projects. When all was said and done, we had spent about $6,000 a year on improvements.

But after a while, I tired of the daily drive from our lake home to civilization. Our closer-to-town location had become not-close-enough-to-town for me. We decided to put the house on the market and were pleasantly surprised when our real estate agent suggested we list it at a price of $284,500. We were more than pleasantly surprised when within 24 hours of putting it on the market, we received an offer of $260,000. We accepted it without making a counteroffer.

You might be wondering if, in hindsight, I think we should have negotiated harder on this point as well. My answer is a resounding no. My husband and I had decided we definitely wanted to move. It was spring, peak season for us to sell and, in turn, find something to buy, and the offer was for more than the minimum price we were willing to accept. In addition, the buyers were purchasing the home as a vacation property. If we had countered, we would have left the door open for them to change their minds about the whole thing. When you need to sell, don't get greedy. A bird in the hand is worth two in the bush.

My husband and I sold our house at the lake for a profit of $110,000. If you take into account the $24,000 we put into the home, the profit was $86,000 (but remember we had also been able to enjoy those improvements while we were living in the house). This was a big money event for us. What we were able to make on that sale was significant and would have taken us quite some time to otherwise accumulate. We purchased our next home for a price of $230,000 ($30,000 less than what we'd sold our lake house for) and were able to easily put a nice down payment on it.

The key to a solid home investment:

differentiation

Do you think of buying a home as making an investment? You should. If you choose wisely, buying a home is one of the best investments you can make. It turns out my husband was definitely right about that house at the lake. Despite its cosmetic flaws, there were several factors about the home that made it an excellent investment. In fact, those cosmetic flaws actually worked in our favor; because of them, we were able to buy the house at a lower price. I'm not suggesting that every house you own is going to generate a six-figure profit in four years. But if you want to put yourself in the position of having the most solid home investment possible, here's what you should be looking for:

$ Location. You know what they say about real estate: location, location, location. This should be your first criteria for finding a solid home investment. Look for an average house (not the biggest or the smallest) in a great location.

$ Unique features. The house should fit into the neighborhood or surrounding area, but it should have some features that are unique or better than the houses around it. I'm not talking about features that can be easily changed, such as granite countertops or stainless steel appliances. I'm talking about distinctive features such as a larger lot, mature landscaping, or waterfront.

$ A "diamond in the rough." Find a house you can improve. This will require some vision on your part, but the payoff can be well worth it. You don't want a house with major structural or mechanical issues. Those kinds of improvements can be very costly. Instead, look for one that can be cosmetically improved. Many buyers want a home that is turn-key ready for them to move into. They want a house they can picture themselves living in as soon as they walk through the door. Find a "diamond in the rough" and turn it into a "turn-key gem."

Once you've purchased your diamond in the rough, one that's in a great location with unique features, you'll probably want to begin implementing your vision right away. But before you do, think frugally. The idea is to put the minimum amount of money into the house that will allow you to get the maximum amount out of it when you decide to sell. Skip the cherry cabinets and Jacuzzi tub, and remember that many things can be taken care of with something as simple as a coat of paint.

Being realistic when buying a home

When it comes time for you to buy a home, whether it be your first or not, you need to engage your frugal mind. Always err on the side of caution when determining your price range. If you have any doubt that you will be able to afford a particular home, even if you love it, even if it makes all the other homes you've looked at pale in comparison, even if it has the three-car garage or fully equipped kitchen you've always wanted, skip it. No home is worth risking your financial future. Many buyers now in foreclosure have told themselves they could afford a certain home, when deep down they knew it would be a struggle.

Let's say you've found a home and you feel comfortable that you can afford it. It's time to put your frugal mind into second gear. Does the home you're looking at meet your needs? I don't mean your need to entertain the entire neighborhood or have a TV room the size of a movie theatre. I'm talking about whether or not it meets the everyday living needs of you and your family. Ask yourself,

"How many times a year would I really use the...?" and fill in the blank. If the answer is only a few times, you can probably live without those extra features and save yourself lots of bucks in the process.

Think about it. Is there a room in your home you never use? Almost everyone has one. Maybe it's the formal living room that you only go into to dust or the dining room that only gets used at Thanksgiving and Christmas. I'm not telling you to buy a house that doesn't have a living room or dining room; what I'm saying is that you should give serious thought to how much space you will really use.

Can you buy a less expensive, smaller home but make full use of all the space? Get creative. Instead of having a living room that resembles a museum—as in, don't touch or sit on anything—make it a functional office. Turn that dining room into a playroom if you've always wanted one, and set up an extra table elsewhere when the holidays roll around.

A bigger home also brings many other expenses with it that people don't often think about. For example, the amount you spend on furnishings, utility bills, remodeling, and repairs will likely increase as your space increases. Don't turn your home purchase into a money pit. If you buy a home in a good location, in a price range you can truly afford, you'll have a solid investment and peace of mind.

The 15-year mortgage

I used to subscribe to the philosophy of some of my financial colleagues when it came to mortgages—the one that says having debt in the form of a mortgage is really no big deal. After all, between the tax deduction for mortgage interest and the low interest rates, a mortgage is some of the cheapest money you'll ever borrow, so why not borrow away? And besides, who would want to sink all of their cash into their house? Then there's no way to get it back, unless you sell or take out a home equity line.

My thinking on mortgages has changed over time. I'm a firm believer that buying a home is a great investment. Hopefully, you made or will make a smart purchase when you buy your home. You'll buy something reasonably priced, in a good location, with something that sets it apart from other properties. In order to make your purchase, you'll take out a mortgage and it'll be some of the cheapest money you'll ever borrow, but that doesn't mean you should borrow it for 30 years. Remember: Debt is still debt, no matter how you slice it.

When you have a mortgage, time is either your friend or your enemy, because your mortgage is potentially a huge roadblock between you and an increased net worth. If you made a smart buy, your house will appreciate in value. You will build equity in your home. Your net worth will increase. Time is on your side. The other way to increase your net worth is to pay down what you owe the bank, and if you take 30 years to do that, time is on the bank's side.

Do the math

If you took out a 30-year mortgage for $200,000 at 3.75 percent, your principal and interest payment would be about $925 per month. At the end of 15 years, you would've only paid off approximately 35 percent of the principal, or about $70,000.

If you took out a 15-year mortgage for $200,000 at 3.25 percent (you'll get a better rate if you finance for a shorter term), your principal and interest payment would be about $1,400. At the end of 15 years, you would have paid off 100 percent of the principal, and would own your home free and clear. Under the second scenario, at the end of 15 years, your net worth would be about $130,000 higher than under the first scenario.

The problem with a 30-year mortgage is that you pay and pay and pay, and never get anywhere. That's a killer to your net worth. In the previous example, you'll pay about $80,000 more in interest on the 30-year mortgage than you would on the 15-year one.

What if you can't pay that extra $470 a month? Then you bought a house you couldn't afford. If you haven't made your purchase yet, only consider homes that you can comfortably make the 15-year mortgage payment on. If you've already purchased a home, start reworking your budget so that you can refinance for 15 years.

A 30-year mortgage is just a smoke screen to convince people to buy houses they can't afford and finance them for longer than they should. Remember: You may be living in your home, but until you pay off that mortgage, you don't really own it.

Buying a vehicle

My advice on the purchase of a vehicle is simple. Buy the cheapest car you can that looks decent and runs well. A car is not an investment. It doesn't increase in value. In fact quite the opposite is true: It loses value over time. According to Edmunds.com, a new car loses 11 percent of its value the minute you drive it off the lot and 15–25 percent per year for the first five years.[1]

A car is an expense and, as such, the smallest amount of debt possible should be incurred for its purchase. Hopefully you can pay cash for it, and no debt will be incurred for its purchase. Search Craigslist.com for good deals from private sellers. Small "mom and pop" used car dealers will often have good deals, too.

I'm not telling you that you have to drive an old beater. Remember: I said "looks decent and runs well," but I'm asking you to buy used for two reasons. First, if you're looking for ways to trim your budget and increase your savings, driving an inexpensive used car can help accomplish those goals. Second, I've seen a lot more people excited that their car is paid for than that they're driving a new one.

That being said, when I mention the words "used car" some of you just aren't going to listen to me. We'll end up in the age-old vehicle debate. This is how it goes: You tell me you're going to buy a new car and that the depreciation doesn't bother you because you're going to drive it forever. Fair enough. If you're really going to drive it forever, then you're demonstrating frugality. I applaud you (and I'll be checking up on you in five years to see if you were telling the truth). Just make sure you don't get sucked into an upgraded model or getting add-on features that can chip away at the thriftiness of your purchase. In addition, if you're buying new and taking out a loan, make sure you're getting a low interest rate. I'm going to give you the benefit of the doubt and make the assumption that you're going to buy a sensibly priced car at a good rate, mostly because I've rarely heard, "I'm going to buy a brand-new Jaguar, but it's okay because I'm going to drive it forever."

Vacations

It can be easy to go over-the-top money-wise when it comes to vacations as well. Remember: The point of a vacation is to spend quality time with your family. If that is your true vacation mission, consider a "staycation." Nothing says quality time like the great outdoors. Pitch a tent in your backyard or check out the campgrounds at your local state parks. You can hike, fish, and swim, all on the cheap. Throw in a few hot dogs and marshmallows, and you've got some serious frugal fun. Make a list of other inexpensive attractions in your local area that you could explore during a staycation.

I realize that for some, sleeping on the ground, eating large amounts of food in buns, and singing a rousing chorus of *Kumbaya* doesn't sound anything like a vacation. If you must head out of town, give yourself plenty of time to research the best deals on things like hotels and airfare. When it comes to hotels, look for properties that are clean but not fancy. You'll want a good location and some basic amenities, but remember that you're not going to be spending that much time in your room.

You should also do some research on free events and attractions around the area you'll be staying. Also, try cutting back on the souvenirs. When you unpack your suitcase, you may start wondering what in the world you were thinking when you just couldn't pass up that seashell purse at the beach or that dancing Elvis doll from Graceland.

Everything is negotiable

You work hard for your money and, especially in these tough economic times, every dollar counts. When it comes to making any purchase, particularly large ones, remember these three words: Everything is negotiable.

Your customer dollars are very precious, to you and to sellers, so always make sure you're getting the absolute best deal possible. From houses to cars to vacations, a smart consumer knows how to get the best price by doing her homework, shopping around, and asking for a discount.

There are a few crucial elements of the negotiation. The first is time. If you are in a hurry to make a purchase, you are not in the best position to negotiate. Sellers can sense when you're eager, and they will use it to their advantage. Ask many questions. Educate yourself on the prices of comparable items or services. Visit several different places that offer what you're looking for. All of these things take time, and the longer you spend debating your purchase, the more anxious the seller will become. Put time on your side and you'll put dollars in your wallet.

The second is power. You have to believe that sellers need your money more than you need what they're selling. When it comes to business transactions, cash is king. If you have the cash, you have the power.

Third, and most importantly, you must be willing to walk away. Before making a purchase, ask yourself these three questions: Do I want it? Do I need it? Do I have to have it?

Even if the answer to the first question is yes, the answer to the second question may or may not be the same. Don't confuse your wants with your needs. You may want a new couch, but it is unlikely that such a purchase is a true need. The answer to the third question is almost always no. Very few things in life are must-haves. If you can recognize that you may want something but don't need or have to have it, you put yourself in the position to walk away.

Negotiating is a skill, one that is best developed through practice. Never be ashamed to bargain. Remember: You're not being cheap; you're being smart. Start practicing now. Those extra dollars in your pocketbook can make a difference in your budget.

7

What Is Net Worth, and Why Should You Care?

A lesson in net worth from Thomas Jefferson

When my older daughter was in fourth grade, I went with her class on a field trip to Monticello, Thomas Jefferson's 5,000-acre plantation located in Charlottesville, Virginia. Touring his home on the mountaintop is a trek that elementary school children all over the state of Virginia make to enhance their social studies curriculum. I have to say, I never took such a big field trip when I was in elementary school and, in fact, I had never been to Monticello before.

As we piled off the bus and headed toward the tour meeting point, it became apparent how extraordinary this home was, especially in its day. We toured each beautifully furnished room on the first floor and took in the extensive book, art, and gadget collections that Jefferson had accumulated. I'm certain that the students were seeing things through the eyes of children. They were very excited by the polygraph machine and most excited about the gift shop. I'm betting the other chaperones were seeing the tour through the eyes of historians, enamored of the historical significance of the home we were touring. I, on the other hand, was looking at Monticello through the eyes of an accountant.

It sounds a little strange, I know, but my interest was piqued when the tour guide mentioned that Jefferson spent most of his life plagued by debt. The principal and interest he owed in his later years became so great that even what he owned was no longer enough to cover it. He had a negative net worth. She didn't exactly say it that way, but that was the bottom line. When Thomas Jefferson died on July 4, 1826, he had accumulated debt that, in today's dollars, would amount to between one and two million dollars.[1] In 1831, his family was forced to sell his possessions, including his gorgeous Monticello, but even the sale of his estate was not enough to cover his debts, and his grandson assumed the remainder.

Jefferson had approximately 10,000 acres of land and a home that was more than 10,000 square feet. He loved wine and gourmet food, and traveled extensively. He was a seemingly wealthy man, but things aren't always what they seem. The third president of the United States, the principal author of the Declaration of Independence, and the founder of the University of Virginia, died flat broke.

Debt was actually very common in colonial days. Planters obtained credit from British merchants to expand their production of commercial crops. If the crops failed, the planters relied on the sale of slaves or land for income. However, as debt in the colonies grew, and because there was not much coin money circulating at that time, it became hard for planters to sell large parcels of their land and stay in a positive net worth position. Thomas Jefferson was no different from other planters of his day. He spent his adult years struggling with debt.

I was shocked to learn that, although a smart man, Jefferson was a financial disaster whose personal finance habits were lacking in multiple ways:

$ **He was an overspender.** As president, Jefferson received a substantial salary of $25,000 per year. However, he had to use this salary to pay for his staff, travel, entertainment, and other incidental expenses. He loved to host dinner parties and serve exceptional food and wine. When Jefferson got ready to retire from the presidency, he realized his expenses had surpassed his salary by $10,000 and he ended up leaving office with a loan for that debt. One would think that after that little snafu, Jefferson would have learned his lesson, but he didn't. He loved stuff, like books, furnishings, and other treasures, and couldn't help but continue to buy and accumulate them. He also continued to build onto and expand Monticello, even though he couldn't afford it.

$ **His farms were not a good investment.** Jefferson thought he could use the salaries from his jobs as minister to France, secretary of state, vice president, and president to pay for his living expenses and use the profit from his farms to pay down his debts. However, farming proved to be an insufficient and undependable source of revenue. Once Jefferson subtracted all of the farming expenses from the total dollars worth of crops he sold, there was barely any profit at all. He continually estimated greater profits than were ever achieved.

$ **He didn't say no frequently enough.** Jefferson co-signed two $10,000 notes for a long-time friend, Wilson Cary Nichols. He felt obligated to do so, because Nichols had done favors for him and because Nichols was also connected to Jefferson's family by marriage. When Nichols died, his estate was not large enough to cover the notes, so Jefferson had to take on the debt himself. In addition, Jefferson loaned money to others whose repayments were undependable and sporadic at best.

$ **He overestimated the value of his assets.** Jefferson came into a significant amount of debt when his wife, Martha Wayles Jefferson, inherited a third of her father's estate. The estate included a large amount of debt owed to British creditors. At that time, the laws were such that the debts could be averted if the estate remained intact until the creditors were paid, but if the assets were divided, the debt followed with them. Jefferson and his two brothers-in-law sized up the estate and felt sure that the sale of some of the land would be enough to pay off the debts. After the Revolutionary War, Jefferson sold his share of the land and the buyers agreed to pay him for it in installments. The purchasers paid the installments with paper money issued during the Revolution that had declined greatly in value but, because of Virginia's wartime legal tender act, Jefferson was required to take it even though he described it as not worth "oak leaves." Later in life, Jefferson was unwilling to sell a significant part of his own land in order to pay off his debts. When the War of 1812 ended, the peace that ensued caused inflated agricultural prices. If Jefferson had been willing to sell during this time and apply the proceeds toward his debts, he may have been able to prevent his financial situation from becoming so dire, but he wouldn't sell. The economic bubble burst, and a recession began that lasted for the rest of his life, causing the value of his assets to decrease.[2]

Jefferson's mistakes can teach us many things about what not to do financially. Jefferson was not a frugal man. He didn't create a balanced budget for himself, he didn't make solid investments, he wasn't assertive with others when it came to money, and he wasn't realistic when he valued his assets. It should provide you with some comfort to know that even a person as accomplished and distinguished as Jefferson was susceptible to making bad financial decisions. Anyone can get themselves into financial trouble. Just think, if you can create a positive net worth or, even better, a high net worth, you'll be more financially savvy than our third president.

What Thomas Jefferson and MC Hammer have in common

No one is immune from the possibility of financial problems. Many celebrities, professional athletes, politicians, CEOs, and other famous individuals have faced financial distress. Although financial disaster can strike in any income bracket, somehow it's even more astonishing when it happens to people who have become rich and famous.

Let's look at another case study of the famous, fabulous, and flat broke. Who could forget MC Hammer? The flashy rap star with those crazy pants used his musical talents and dance skills to earn a whopping $33 million from his music career. Then he used extremely poor judgment to build an extravagant $12 million home with $2 million worth of Italian marble, a 17-car garage (for his 17 automobiles, of course), and two helicopters. The monthly wages he paid for his entourage of more than 300 people totaled more than $500,000. He blew through his

$33 million and then some, and in 1996 found himself in bankruptcy court, rather than in his cushy 33-seat home movie theater. In 1997, he sold his enormous mansion, which was also an enormously bad investment, for $5.3 million.[3]

Hammer is just one more example of someone who was wealthy, yet spent and lost everything. There are many more. Rembrandt Harmenszoon van Rijn is considered one of the greatest artists in European history. He was an extraordinary painter and printmaker. However, Rembrandt was also an overspender. He bought art, antiques, and other collectibles, and in 1656, at age 50, had to file bankruptcy. His assets including his paintings, prints, house, and antiques had to be sold at auction.

In 1894, Samuel Clemens, best known under the pen name Mark Twain, filed for bankruptcy. Although he authored brilliant writings such as *Tom Sawyer* and *The Adventures of Huckleberry Finn,* and made a considerable amount of money doing so, he spent most of it on bad investments. Twain spent what would be equivalent to approximately $7 million in today's dollars investing in the Paige typesetting machine, but the machine frequently broke down and the investment became unsuccessful. Even after he declared bankruptcy, he was committed to repaying his debts and, after going on a world lecture tour, did just that.

Bud Post won a $16.2 million lottery jackpot in 1988. He blew through the entire amount buying houses, cars, trucks, motorcycles, campers, boats, and electronics. Eight years after he won the big prize, he had to declare bankruptcy due to his constant spending. In 2006, he died with no significant net worth.

Mike Tyson is one of the best-known boxers in history. He was the youngest man to ever win the world heavyweight title and received $30 million for a single fight. He earned an estimated $300 million during his boxing career, but also lived an extravagant lifestyle that was reported to have cost about $400,000 a month. In 2003, Tyson declared bankruptcy.

In 2006, Suge Knight, co-founder and former CEO of Death Row Records (a company that signed multi-platinum artists Dr. Dre, Snoop Dogg, and Tupac), filed for bankruptcy. He made millions of dollars from Death Row, but at the time he filed, he had $11 in his bank account and was forced to sell his home.[4]

Gary Busey, Randy Quaid, and Toni Braxton, who actually filed for bankruptcy twice, are just a few more of the many celebrities who have gone bust.[5] The list goes on and on.

So what can we learn from those who lived the lifestyle of the rich and famous, only to become infamous for their lack of good money management?

First, in order to be truly wealthy, you can't just have things; you must own them. There's a big difference. Do you own the title to your home, or do you have a mortgage on it? Do you own your car, or do you have a car loan? In order to be in the best financial position, it is very important to pay off your debt, thus reducing your liabilities.

Second, you must choose your assets wisely. An asset is only worth what someone else will actually pay for it, not what you hope someone will pay for it. In 1831, Monticello and 522 surrounding acres sold for $7,000, around $180,000 in today's dollars.[6]

Third, you must hang onto your assets by making wise financial decisions, including making good investment decisions and not overspending.

Don't learn these financial lessons the hard way, the way MC Hammer and others like him did. Make yourself a success. Then work hard to stay successful. In the end, if you let net worth be your guide, you'll always be on the right track

The nuts and bolts of net worth

Net worth is the number you want to focus on during your financial journey. It's the most accurate indicator of your true wealth. But everybody already knows what it means to be wealthy, right? It means you've got a lot of stuff, a huge house, an expensive car, and maybe a summer home. Not necessarily true. Net worth is calculated by taking your total assets minus your total liabilities. In other words, it's what you own minus what you owe. Many people believe that if they have things like a big house and a fancy car, then they are wealthy and others will view them as wealthy, but they gloss over the liabilities portion of the net worth equation. If your assets are more than your liabilities, you have a positive net worth. If your liabilities are more than your assets, you have a negative net worth. Net worth is the truest wealth gauge, because it takes into account both the actual value of your assets and the obligations that exist against them.

Banks and other lenders will often want to see a calculation of your net worth before they'll loan you money. If you have a negative net worth, you'll be considered a credit risk. You'll likely find it more difficult to get a loan, and your interest rate will not be as good. The higher your net worth, the better your chance of getting the lowest possible rate.

To calculate your net worth, first add up the value of all your assets. Don't fool yourself by overinflating their value. They should be valued at their actual current market value not the price you paid for them and not what you wish they were worth. Your assets will include your:

$ Home. If you own your home, include its current market value. You can get this information from a recent appraisal or the assessment of a real estate agent, or you can do some research of your own on recent sales of comparable homes in your area. You may also be able to use your tax assessment although, depending on how recently your property was assessed, this may or may not accurately reflect your home's current value.

$ Other real estate. This should be the current market value of any other real estate you own. This includes other homes, land, and rental and commercial property. Use the same sources you used for your home to gather the current value information for your other real estate.

$ Vehicles. Include the current market value of any vehicles you own, such as cars, trucks, motorcycles, boats, and so on. Websites such as Kelley Blue Book can help you determine the current value of your vehicles.

$ Jewelry. Include the current market value of rings, necklaces, earrings, pins, loose stones, and so forth. To determine the current market value of your jewelry, take it to a local certified appraiser.

$ Household goods. This includes furniture, electronics, glassware, dishware, and so on. Be realistic when estimating the current value of these items. Think of their value in terms of how much you could sell them for on Craigslist, not what you paid for them.

$ Retirement accounts. This should be the value of any pensions, 401(k)s, 403(b)s, IRAs, and any other retirement accounts you have. Check your account statements to get the current balance of your accounts.

$ Stocks, bonds, and mutual funds. Include the current value of these securities. Check your account statement or use the stock ticker symbol to check the current share price online.

$ Cash. Include the balance in your checking, savings, money market accounts, CDs, and any other cash you have on hand.

Now, add up the value of all your liabilities. Your liabilities include your:

$ Mortgages. Include the balance on your home mortgage as well as any other mortgages on other real estate you own. You should also include the balances on any second mortgages or home equity lines. You can call the mortgage company to get the exact payoff for your loan.

$ Vehicle loans. This is the total amount you owe on your vehicles. Again, you can call the loan company to get an exact payoff.

$ Student loans. Include the balance on any outstanding student loans you have.

$ Credit card debt. This should be the total balance on all credit cards you have.

$ Other debt. Include any other debts you owe.

Subtract your liabilities from your assets to arrive at your total net worth. Thus, Assets – Liabilities = Net Worth. Do you want to know how your net worth stacks up in comparison to others your age? CNN Money's net worth calculator shows the following median net worth by age[7]:

Younger than 25	**$1,475**
25–34	$8,525
35–44	$51,575
45–54	$98,350
55–64	$180,125
65 and older	**$232,000**

Now that you've calculated your current net worth, doing a future net-worth projection can give you a good road map of where you need to go financially. It can also help you solidify your financial goals and find the motivation to achieve them. There are two things you can do to positively affect your net worth: increase your assets and decrease your liabilities.

First, do a projection of what your assets will look like at the end of the year for each of the next five years.

$ Your home and other real estate. Add an appreciation percentage to the current market value of your properties. Because real estate appreciation varies greatly by local area, you should consult a local real estate agent to find out what kind of appreciation your area typically experiences. This is why it's also important to make a smart purchase, as discussed in Chapter 5. If you make an intelligent buy, you will get higher than average appreciation.

$ Vehicles. Unfortunately, unless you own collector cars, your vehicles will not appreciate; they will depreciate. Remember: A new car loses 15–25 percent per year for the first five years. After that, you can estimate the miles you will put on your vehicle and use a Website like Kelley Blue Book to determine how the value of your vehicle will continue to be affected.

$ Retirement accounts, stocks, bonds, and mutual funds. Hopefully, your investments in these categories will grow each year for two reasons. First, you will be contributing more money to them each year, and second, you will see a return on your investments each year. If you look at your account online, it should provide you with the average annual rate of return for the last one-, three-, and five-year periods for the stocks, bonds, or mutual funds that your money is invested in. Use this information to determine what your investments will be worth in the future.

$ Jewelry and household goods. Unless you own some highly collectible items, you are not going to see much appreciation on your jewelry and household goods. In fact, the pace at which new technology develops make household goods like electronics out-of-date and less valuable very quickly. Furniture, appliances, and other household goods also depreciate over time. This is why you have to engage your frugal mind before making these kinds of purchases, so you can be sure to keep this use of your money in check.

$ Cash. Your cash category will grow based on the amount you contribute to savings each year. In addition, you will also see a small amount of appreciation based on the interest rate of your checking, savings, or money market account, or CD.

When you're projecting the future value of your assets, don't forget to take into account the beauty of compounding. Compounding results when interest is added on top of your principal, and then that interest earns interest, too. Compounding also applies to the return on your investments, such as your 401(k). You can see how the power of compounding will make your money grow more quickly. You can also see why you need to start investing as early as possible, so you can maximize the benefit of compounding.

Do the math

Beginning balance in your 401(k) account = $30,000.

After looking at your account information online, you determine that the average annual rate of return on the funds that your 401(k) is invested in is 6.5 percent. (The following amounts have been rounded to the nearest dollar.)

At the end of the first year, your account will be worth $30,000 + ($30,000 × .065) or $31,950.

At the end of the second year, your account will be worth $31,950 + ($31,950 × .065) or $34,027.

At the end of the third year, your account will be worth $34,027 + ($34,027 × .065) or $36,239.

At the end of the fourth year, your account will be worth $36,239 + ($36,239 × .065) or $38,595.

At the end of the fifth year, your account will be worth $38,595 + ($38,595 × .065) or $41,104.

In addition, let's say you plan to contribute $500 per month to your 401(k) account for the next five years. At the end of the first year, your balance would be $38,159. By the end of the fifth year, your balance would be $76,456.

Over the course of 20 to 30 years, the power of compounding will have an even more profound effect on your net worth. If you continued to contribute $500 per month and earn a 6.5 percent return, your account balance would be $734,751 at the end of 30 years. Be sure to factor anticipated interest rates or rates of return and contributions, where applicable, into your future asset calculations.

Second, once you've completed projection of your assets, project what your liabilities will look like at the end of the year for the next five years. Remember: Don't get hung up on which one you pay off first. Just get down to the business of lowering those balances.

When you're calculating the projected liability reduction on loans such as your mortgage and car, remember to reduce debt balances by only the principal portion of your payment, not by the entire payment. For example, if you owe $225,000 on your mortgage and the monthly payment is $1,800, don't multiply $1,800 by 12 and subtract it from the $225,000 to project what the balance will be a year from now. Instead, subtract only the principal portion of each of the 12 payments from $225,000 to calculate the balance. When you signed for your loan, the bank should have given you an amortization schedule that shows what portion of each payment is principal and what portion is interest.

Creating a five-year net-worth plan is a great way to get a big-picture look at your finances. Hopefully, this exercise will convince you to put your extra dollars into lowering liabilities rather than making more purchases. In addition, it should be a reality check on what you should put your money into and what you shouldn't when making purchases. Most "stuff" depreciates. Put your money into things that are going to increase your net worth. You don't want to be a person who has everything they've got out on the showroom floor. Rather, be a person who has real wealth in the bank and in good investments. Remember: True wealth isn't always apparent to the people around you.

Your greatest asset, your greatest liability

Take a minute and look at the asset section of your current net worth calculation. What is your greatest asset—your house, car, or pension? Now look at the liability section. What is your greatest liability—your mortgage, car loan, or credit card debt?

I'm going to let you in on a little financial secret. The answer to both of these questions is you. That's right. You are your greatest asset. You are your greatest liability. Make this your new mantra. You have to believe it in order to be successful financially.

Let's revisit the MC Hammer example. Hammer was talented—talented enough to own a recording business, sell more than 50 million records, and win three Grammy Awards. He catapulted himself from a rough section of East Oakland into the glow of the entertainment spotlight. He was his greatest asset. Then he let his spending get out of control. He was now his greatest liability.

It's much easier to take credit for your successes than to own your failures. When we're successful, we pat ourselves on the back. We attribute it to our hard work, our intelligence, and our expertise in our field. When we experience failure, however, it's easier for us to deflect the blame onto someone or something else, rather than analyze our role in it. We feel as if the stars were just lined up against us and say things like "It isn't fair," and "I have terrible luck."

Take personal responsibility for all of your financial actions, good and bad. Embrace your role in both your successes and failures, and know that most of the things that happen to us in life financially, both positive and negative, are directly attributable to our own actions. The key to an increased net worth is an awareness of your financial weaknesses and a belief that you can be successful financially. I'm not suggesting that you can just sit around and wish yourself into riches. That won't happen. But have faith in the fact that if you really want to be successful financially, you can. The choice is yours. Anyone who has accomplished a major life goal knows that it doesn't come without sacrifice. There will be times when you doubt yourself, when you think that you don't really have what it takes to obtain a high net worth. You'll doubt your willpower, your ability to make money, and your ability to save money. You'll begin to think that it's never going to happen for you, but with patience, persistence, and commitment, it will happen.

Begin investing in yourself the way you would in your savings account, home, or 401(k). Your intangible assets, such as your knowledge, skills, and determination, are what will truly transform you financially. Remember: There are two ways you can boost your net worth. You can increase your assets, and you can decrease your liabilities.

Commit to continually looking for ways to increase your assets. Ask yourself hard questions, such as: What can I do to increase my income? Give your job 110 percent each day to put yourself in the best possible position for raises and promotions. No matter what line of work you're in, you always have customers. Those customers might be internal "customers" like your managers and coworkers, or they might be external customers who are purchasing goods and services from you. Make sure you're giving your customers 110 percent each day so that word will spread and your income will grow. Look into additional training or coursework you could take to make yourself more marketable. If you are capable of earning an income, you are capable of earning a better income. Then you must make good decisions with it. Get some financial education to learn how to make better investments. At the same time, start decreasing your liabilities. Pay off your debt, and commit to remaining debt free.

Your finances are limited only by you. Whether you have squandered your assets through overspending, not taken the steps necessary to increase your income, or chosen to live financially uneducated, the choice has been yours. The thing holding you back is you.

You can blame the economy, the stock market, the politicians, and a whole host of other people and circumstances for that fact that your net worth isn't where you'd like it to be, but that won't get you anywhere. Taking action will. Taking back your financial responsibility means taking back the power to control your financial fate.

Don't be your own worst enemy. Align your actions with your financial goals. If you make it a priority to increase your assets and simultaneously decrease your liabilities, you will be well on your way to an increased net worth.

8

Income: A Crucial Part of the Financial Equation

A lesson in income from my chicken farming days

When we purchased our 100-year-old farmhouse, we loved that it had many quaint features, but one I was particularly enamored of was the chicken coop out back. If you think there couldn't possibly be anything charming about a chick coop, let me tell you, this one was just adorable. Painted white with blue trim, a chicken palace really, it had been built from the ground up by the previous owners.

Visions of chickens began dancing in my head, and in no time at all, I had ordered 26 female feathered friends online from the Murray McMurray Hatchery. I waited anxiously for my eight Rhode Island Reds, eight Black Australorps, nine Pearl White Leghorns, and one free mystery chick to arrive. Several visits to the feed–and–seed followed to stock up on food, waterers, and grit.

When I finally got the call from the post office to come pick them up, I was so excited, it didn't even faze me that it was 5 a.m. As I walked in and rang the special before-hours doorbell, I was hoping the postman would be nice enough to help me carry my large box out to the car. What a fool I felt like when he handed me my peeping package, not much larger than a shoebox. Day-old chicks don't take up much space and I later learned they purposely pack 'em in tight for warmth.

The baby chicks were so cute. We held them, took pictures with them, and counted them, and realized we had 27 instead of 26. You know what they say: Everyone loves a chick.

But at a rapid pace, those chicks turned into chickens. As the days passed, it became clear our mystery chick and our extra chick were roosters. All the better I thought, still filled with optimism. The sound of a rooster crowing at dawn was just the sort of ambience I was yearning for. And beyond that, the hens were reaching laying age. It was such a thrill to head out to the coop each morning in hopes of finding the first egg.

The first egg came all right, and many more after. Twenty-five hens lay a lot of eggs, and pretty soon our refrigerator was overflowing. That's when the CPA in me took over, and my visions of chickens turned into visions of dollars. We could sell eggs to all the neighbors. We could sell them to the local food store. We could sell them at the farmer's markets. I set to creating labels for our cartons. "Levison Farm," they read. I was so proud when the local food store told me they would pay $1.80 per dozen; I felt like the most savvy entrepreneur on the planet.

Every Monday morning, I would fill up a large plastic storage tub, haul my eggs off to the store, and rake in my approximately 25-dollar check. In addition, the neighbors were calling to pick up a dozen here and there, bringing my grand total per week to about 30 dollars.

It wasn't until I realized what chickens do even better than lay eggs that my optimism began to fade. And what they do better than anything else is poop. There was poop on the ground, on the walkway, and on the porch. And believe me, there's nothing charming about that. Runner-up to pooping is scratching, so my flower beds were in a constant state of upheaval. If that wasn't bad enough, the fence around the chicken coop might as well have been non-existent. The gusto with which my chickens flew right over it to wreak their havoc was amazing, and eventually I was faced with only one solution: "clipping."

Late one night, my husband and my father snuck out to the coop and, one by one, clipped the wings of the roosting chickens. If you're beginning to mull over the ethical issues involved in clipping a chicken's wings, let me save you some trouble. It's like cutting fingernails. They will grow back, and about 10 of them were never affected a bit. They were still flying right over the fence. A week later, the men went out to see if they could trim some more. They cut as much as humanely possible, and still my chickens flew the coop.

This was beginning to wear on me, as was the packing of eggs and the driving to the store to get my 25 dollars. It's at this point that I should probably mention I actually have a bird phobia, so the chickens were starting to creep me out. I was beginning to ponder whether or not this was really worth the pittance I was getting from the egg sales, but I had no choice. My refrigerator just couldn't hold all those eggs.

Then one Monday morning, my husband had the day off work and went with me to the local food store to make my sale. The parking lot there was very steep and rather difficult to maneuver, and before I knew it, he had backed into another car. After taking into account the increased insurance premiums we had to pay when the other driver turned in the claim, my venture was now severely in the red.

Just as I was reaching the point of desperation, I received a call from a woman who had bought my eggs at the local store. She wanted to know if I had any chicks for sale. No, thank God, was my first thought, but then I offered to give her all of my chickens that could still fly over the fence. "I've had enough," I told her. "If they're flyers, they're fryers." So she happily took them off my hands.

I have to admit that, in the beginning, my husband did most of the chicken work. He fed them, he watered them, and he let them out in the morning to roam their yard and shut the coop door each night so predators couldn't get in. But now he was traveling for work more frequently, and the chicken duties began to fall on my shoulders. The last straw was very near.

I had taken my daughters to school and daycare, and was on my way to work when it dawned on me that I had forgotten to let the chickens out. It was a hot summer day, and I hated to think of them being cooped up for hours, so I swung by the house to give them their freedom. A chicken coop, it turns out, is a yucky little place no matter how cute it may look from the outside. I also hated opening the door, because all those flapping feathers would nearly give me a panic attack. I stepped up into the coop, released the hook that was keeping the small chicken door closed, and turned to make my quick exit. As I stepped down, my ankle twisted underneath me and I fell flat on my back out into the yard. It all happened so fast. It was only after I was sure I hadn't completely broken my ankle that I realized I was lying in a dress and high heels surrounded by a ground full of chicken poop. I dragged myself over to the fence to assess the situation. My ankle was sore and very swollen, and on top of that, it was obvious I was going to need to take another shower.

That was my last day as a chicken farmer. The chicken door never got closed at night again and pretty soon nature took its course and the local wildlife took care of my chicken problem.

The problem with my chicken farm side business was that in reality it turned out to be just a hobby, and not a very fun one at that. It never ended up generating any income. It was a lot of work, but it didn't make me any money. In order to be successful financially, one of your most basic goals should be to have a livable income. Then you can work on increasing your assets by continuing to increase that income. One of the ways you can do that is through alternative ventures that are actually profitable.

Detrimental career profiles

Income is a crucial part of your financial equation. Remember: You improve your net worth when you increase your assets and decrease your liabilities. One essential way to increase your assets is through your income. The more income you have, the more you have to save and invest.

There are several career profiles that can be absolutely detrimental to you generating more income. The first is the unrealistic entrepreneur. Unrealistic entrepreneurs are usually in pursuit of a job that will enable them to make more and work less. Therefore, they view working for themselves as an ideal situation. They decide to give up on the daily grind, leaving all that accountability and structure behind, and find an endeavor where they can make their own hours, be their own boss, and answer to no one. Being entrepreneurial is a wonderful thing, but those who are successful at it will tell you it is not less work. Successful entrepreneurs pour their heart and soul into their businesses, working long hours to ensure its growth.

Do the math

On average, small business owners work 52 hours per week. Sixty-two percent report working 50 or more hours per week, 57 percent report working six or more days per week, and only 7 percent say they work fewer than five days per week.[1]

In order to generate income through an entrepreneurial venture, you need a solid business plan, not a fantasy. Do I believe anything is possible if you just set your mind to it? Absolutely, I do. I'm sure someone somewhere is very successful at chicken farming, like that guy who founded Perdue, but I also feel sure he had a more solid plan than I did. A plan is crucial, but I was just flying on a wing and a prayer.

According to the U.S. Small Business Administration, roughly 50 percent of all small businesses fail within the first five years.[2] Creating a solid business plan will help ensure that you're not one of them.

I did a lot of things wrong when it came to chicken farming, but the one thing I did right was recognize that the chicken farm was a dream. It sounded like a nice idea, but I really knew very little about it. I thank my lucky stars I didn't quit the accounting job I already had to go into chicken farming full-time. Although I have to admit, I was delusional enough in the beginning to let the thought enter my mind a few times.

It's not that I don't want you to pursue your dreams. I just want you to recognize that often the pursuit of a dream is a long-term goal and one that usually requires funding from a regular day job. If your dream venture requires additional education or experience, you should work on acquiring it, but in the here and now, you must also have a steady income.

The second profile is that of the continual job hopper. The job hopper is in constant pursuit of the elusive better job. Job hoppers believe they will be able to obtain a better position somewhere else, one at a higher rank or pay level, even though they have not fully established themselves in their current one. When the going gets tough, job hoppers are on to the next thing. But often the grass isn't greener on the other side, and job hoppers usually trade security for uncertainty. Because they are usually looking for a job that is less work and pays more, many of them turn into unrealistic entrepreneurs.

———

According to a survey by the Bureau of Labor Statistics, people born between 1957 and 1964 held an average of 11 jobs between the ages of 18 and 44.[3] How does the frequency of your job changes compare to this?

If you've found yourself in the job-hopper category, it's time to have your wings clipped. Especially in today's job market, trading security for uncertainty can be a big mistake.

Arnold H. Glasgow said, "The key to everything is patience. You get the chicken by hatching the egg, not by smashing it."[4] Job success requires the ability to stick it out in good times and in bad. The way to move up is by proving yourself to be promotable. You can't do that if you never stick around long enough for people to see what kind of worker you are.

In addition, future employers are going to wonder what they're getting themselves into if you have a resume that includes five different jobs during the last two years. This will make you look unstable, undependable, and perhaps difficult to work with. These are not characteristics an employer is looking for.

Sometimes there will be a legitimate reason for changing jobs. For instance, if you're working one of the "any job is better than no job" positions and you receive a job offer in your area of expertise, then definitely take it and move on. But if you're working at a job that matches your qualifications, stick it out for at least a year; anything less than that doesn't give you enough time to determine whether it's a good fit or not.

Third, we have the eternal student. These folks have made a career out of pursuing degrees. Unfortunately, this career generates income of zero dollars per hour. Education is a wonderful thing. The pursuit of knowledge is admirable. But there's a difference between lifelong learning and being a lifelong college student. Eventually, you must be able to translate your education into a job that's going to earn income. The reality is that education is expensive and if you've found yourself in a state of perpetual "studentism," you're doing a double whammy on your finances. You're sending money out the door, while bringing none in. Higher education should be the short-term means to obtaining good long-term income.

———

Published in-state tuition and fees at public four-year institutions averaged $8,655 in 2012–13. $8,655 per year × 4 years = $34,620.[5]

If you decide you want to make this kind of investment, you should continue to work at your job while doing it, and many companies offer tuition assistance benefits. In addition, make sure your investment has a return of, at most, four years. That means when you are finished with your additional degree, you should be able to earn an additional $8,655 per year in salary, so your degree will have paid for itself after four years.

Finally, we have the endlessly unemployed. Unless you are independently wealthy, a job is numero uno, the letter A in the alphabet, the first rung of the ladder. You get the picture. You can't sit around all day waiting for the bucks to come rolling in. The endlessly unemployed sometimes come up with all kinds of excuses for not having a job. They blame it on the economy. They blame it on their last employer. They blame it on the weather forecast for the next month. Or, my favorite, they're holding out for a management position.

The average unemployment benefit is approximately $300 per week.[6]

$10 per hour × 40 hours = $400 per week.

If you take a job paying just $10 per hour, you come out ahead by $100 per week, and this doesn't even factor in the value of other benefits such as insurance and paid time off. In addition, you have to start somewhere and at least get your foot in the door. You don't have any chance of working your way up if you're not working at all.

I know what you may be thinking: "The national unemployment rate is hovering around 8 percent. More than 12 million workers are unemployed.[7] We're still in the midst of an economic crisis, and she thinks we can just stop making excuses and go get a job?" In one word, yes; this is America, the greatest country on earth, the land of opportunity.

I realize there are many of you that are currently unemployed and have no desire to bask in the glow of the boob tube all day. You're trying. You're sending out resumes. And you're still coming up short. What then is my advice for you? It's time to resort to the "any job is better than no job" list.

Right before the holidays, a friend of mine found himself unemployed. He'd been the manager of the same company for many years, but just as St. Nick was about to come down the chimney, my pal received an early present: a pink slip. What do you think he did, faced with this situation? He filled out 30 applications at places of business, ranging from grocery stores to local government offices, and landed a job in no time as a cook at a local restaurant. Many people wouldn't have even applied for such a job, considering it far below the level of their education and experience, but my friend took whatever he could get. Then he showed up on time, with a great attitude, and accomplished more in the first four hours than his boss thought he would all day. By the end of the first week, he was in the management program.

Starting over is tough, there's no doubt about it. You went to school, perhaps even attained post-graduate degrees. You have years of experience and expertise in your field. You don't want to settle for a lesser position. Don't think of it as settling. Think of it as being a responsible citizen and family member, a contributor.

Lowering your standards can evoke feelings of unfairness. And maybe it isn't fair, but sometimes you have no other choice. Be proud that you're doing whatever it takes to put food on the table, and think of yourself as a hard worker, no matter what kind of work you're doing.

If you fit any of the detrimental career profiles I've described, make a change. The cycle they create is one of financial distress. If you are an unrealistic entrepreneur, job hopper, eternal student, or endlessly unemployed, start making a better career plan that will result in increased income.

Network

You should be networking every day. They say your net worth is equal to your network, and this is often true. Networking is like an insurance policy on your current income situation. If that situation changes, networking should help you sleep easier at night. It also allows you to make valuable connections that can be tapped into when you need them. The funny thing about networking is that you never know when and where you're going to meet someone that might be able to help you increase your income, but I guarantee that if you keep putting yourself out there, you'll come across many of these people.

Begin integrating your networking skills into daily life. Whether you're at a meeting, conference, or social event, make it a point to seek out at least one person you don't know and introduce yourself. Exchange information with them.

Everyone should have a business card. This card should contain at minimum your name, title or brief description of what kind of work you do, and contact information such as phone number and e-mail address. Even if it's basic, the business card is a powerful networking tool.

Online social media has also become a powerful networking tool. Sites such as Facebook, Twitter, and LinkedIn can help you make beneficial connections. Use them as an important part of your networking strategy, but remember they are not a substitute for face-to-face interaction.

Your spouse's income

I would be remiss if I didn't touch on one final word about income, and it goes like this. If you're dependent on your spouse's income, being married is now your full-time job.

I'm a firm believer that every able-bodied adult should have a career, and I have no problem with women or men who have chosen homemaker as theirs. However, this is another career that generates income of zero dollars per hour, and though I realize you can't put a price on raising a child or assisting an elderly parent, I've seen many women become trapped in an unhappy marriage because they felt like they had no way of supporting themselves financially.

As housewives (or househusbands—I realize you're out there, too), you've already created a plan that led you to the career of your choice. Now I'd encourage you to create a Plan B. Hopefully you'll never have to act on Plan B, but you just never know. Whether it be due to illness, death, divorce, or some other unforeseen circumstances, every person needs to be prepared to stand on his or her own two financial feet.

Alternative ways to increase your income

Here are some things you can do beyond working the traditional 9-to-5 job that can help bring in some extra income:

$ **Sell stuff.** Websites like eBay and Craigslist have made it easy to sell anything from clothes to cars to a wide market of people, all from the comfort of your own home. Get rid of those things big and small that you no longer need or use. If you're a thrift store connoisseur, you can also pick things up inexpensively and then sell them for a profit.

$ **Contract or freelance work.** Freelance work used to be primarily thought of for journalists, writers, and photographers. But these days, with companies trying to cut costs by hiring workers that don't require benefits, a wide variety of jobs can be done freelance. If you already have a regular full-time job, contract out your skills on a moonlighting basis. If you're currently a stay-at-home parent, working on a contract basis can be particularly appealing. It can allow you to bring in some extra income while also providing a good deal of flexibility.

$ **Give lessons.** Is there something you're good at that would be of value to others? Do you play the piano or speak a foreign language, or can you tutor a certain subject? If so, consider giving lessons to others either in their home or yours.

$ **Do odd jobs.** Can you provide lawncare, childcare, pet-sitting, or house cleaning services? Start by advertising in your neighborhood, where people will know and trust you. Then, expand your service area as you work on building your client list.

$ **Trade services.** If your neighbor needs lawncare and you need child care, instead of paying for these services, make a trade. Trading is mutually beneficial. Both parties can get something they want without putting out any cash for it.

$ **Pick up a regular second job.** Think about jobs that are conducive to night and weekend work.

Consider waiting tables or bartending, where you have the potential to increase your hourly income substantially through tips during peak times.

These are a few ways to increase your income. If you get creative, I'm sure you can think of more. But remember: These alternative ideas should be used as income supplements. They aren't a substitute for a livable income coming into your household; rather, they are ways of enhancing it.

I'm challenging you to take action and make income mediocrity unacceptable in your household. No matter what your current income may be, there's always room for improvement. When it comes to earning potential, don't let the line between "I can't" and "I won't" become blurred. Put yourself in the best possible position for promotions by being so great at your job that your boss would be a complete fool not to recognize your star potential. Go above and beyond each day to make yourself stand out to your employer and your customers. Then, find ways to supplement your regular income. All of these things will help you increase your assets by increasing your income.

9

Wanting to Be Rich Doesn't Make You Evil

A lesson about the quest from corporate

America

I've worked in corporate America for more than a decade now. I started there right out of college, and the journey has taught me many lessons. Some of them are less meaningful in the grand scheme of life, like how important an office with a window is to a lot of people or the value of a really well done quad chart. But working in a corporate environment also taught me that embarking on a quest for increased wealth isn't a bad thing. In fact, it's pretty good goal.

I met the man who would become my husband my first day on the job. He was actually the first person I saw when

I walked into the lobby, and I think it really might have been love at first sight. He was working in contracts, and I had been hired for accounting. Pretty soon the other employees noticed him hanging around my office—or should I say my cubicle with no window—quite a bit. As the rumor mill started churning, I began to find out that a few of the other employees weren't as head over heels about him as I was. They thought he was a corporate climber with his eye on creating a name for himself and moving up the ladder. Guess what? He was. Truth be told, it was one of things I liked about him. He was hard-working and ambitious. In my book, these are positive characteristics, but when people are jealous or insecure with their own position in life, they find ambitious people threatening.

Eight months after I first walked into that lobby, I married that industrious man, and the rest, as they say, is history. Corporate America began rewarding his go-getter attitude, and my husband did, in fact, begin climbing the ladder. He moved from contracts to operations, which came with long hours and lots of phone calls in the middle of the night. He moved from operations to programs, then to business development, which came with longer hours and lots of travel. But through time, he made an excellent career for himself and income for our family.

As for me, I was working on climbing the ladder, too, but after the birth of my second daughter, I told my boss I wanted to work part-time, which was basically unheard of in the company at that point. Fortunately for me, I had made myself an asset to my department. I was a team player and someone my boss could count on. I got the job done quickly and correctly. I brought my "A game" every day when I was working full-time, so they decided they wanted me to stay, even if it was only part-time.

My husband and I were working hard for our money, but we were not slaves to it. Money does not enslave you. Money frees you. It gives you the freedom to buy a home, to make investments, to save for the future. Because my husband was making a good salary, money gave me the freedom to work part-time and spend more time with my daughters.

Was my husband cold and shallow because he was on a quest for financial success? A few people had tried to tell me that, but I never bought it. And you shouldn't either. I'm not trying to convince you that money is the most important thing in life, but I am going to try to convince you that money is not the root of all evil. Now before you write me off as a wealth monger who worships at the altar of the corporate idol, let me tell you the rest of the story.

Life was going quite nicely for us in corporate America, when we found out that our company had lost a major contract. Suddenly everything became very uncertain, as layoffs loomed on the horizon. It was a difficult time. Many people began finding jobs elsewhere. Every week, we would hear the names of more people who were leaving. One of my coworkers started keeping a spreadsheet to track it, because the list of names began to get so long. People who had worked together for years were routinely saying good-bye to each other.

We had daily discussions about the state of affairs at work. In fact, it seemed that the uncertainty was all we could talk about. We spent much time speculating and commiserating. But no conversation stuck with me as much as one I had with a coworker who began working with the company long before I had.

If there's one lesson I've learned during my time in corporate America, it's that no one is irreplaceable. I've seen many people come and go over the years. Some had risen high in the management ranks. Some had specialized knowledge. Sometimes we wondered how we would make it without them, but we always did. The corporate machine always keeps cranking. One clown doesn't stop the circus.

As we discussed this phenomenon and how it would surely be the case even with our current situation, my coworker told me that working in corporate America was like sticking your hand in a bucket of water. When you pull it out, there are a few ripples at first but the next thing you know, it's as if your hand was never even there. Saxon N. White Kessinger wrote about this in his poem "There Is No Indispensable Man."

I'm an advocate of ambition. I think it's admirable to want more, and I believe success is something that should be celebrated. But I also believe that most people want to make a meaningful mark on the world. They want to leave a legacy of something beyond wealth.

People leave their legacies in different ways. Some, like Steve Jobs, do leave a corporate legacy, but those are rare. Most leave a legacy through their children and their charity. In order to lead a balanced life, you should be ambitious and charitable. Because of our ambitions, my husband and I have been able to donate our time and our money. We've supported our church, our alma mater, wildlife conservation efforts, and various local causes that we feel strongly about. I've had the opportunity to volunteer as PTA president, Girl Scout leader, and Sunday School teacher.

Money is not your enemy; it is your friend. Money helps you, and it helps you help others. When you have more money, you have more to share. When you're not spending your time stressing over your finances, you have more time to share. When you combine the two, you help ensure that when you pull your hand out of the bucket, people will remember you were there.

Money: The root of all evil?

Money is the root of all evil. Isn't that an interesting saying? According to the *Random House Dictionary of America's Popular Proverbs and Sayings*, "Money is the root of all evil" is a phrase that first appeared in English around 1000 AD. It has its origins in the New Testament: "For the love of money is the root of all evil: which while some coveted after, they have erred from the faith, and pierced themselves through with many sorrows" (1 Timothy 6:10, KJV).

Whether you believe that money is the root of all evil or that the love of money is the root of all evil, I believe that money is a reward for hard work, maturity, and intelligence. Money is a tool you can use to make wonderful things happen for you, your family, and others that are deserving. You have to believe in the virtues of money in order to be successful with it.

Here are two of my favorite excerpts from Francisco's "money speech" in Ayn Rand's novel *Atlas Shrugged*. They are by far the most eloquent presentation of the virtues of money that I've come across.

"So you think that money is the root of all evil?" said Francisco d'Anconia. "Have you ever asked what is the root of money? Money is a tool of exchange, which can't exist unless there are goods produced and men able to produce them. Money is the material shape of the principle that men who wish to deal with one another must deal by trade and give value for value. Money is not the tool of the moochers, who claim your product by tears, or of the looters, who take it from you by force. Money is made possible only by the men who produce. Is this what you consider evil?

"Or did you say it's the love of money that's the root of all evil? To love a thing is to know and love its nature. To love money is to know and love the fact that money is the creation of the best power within you, and your passkey to trade your effort for the effort of the best among men. It's the person who would sell his soul for

a nickel, who is loudest in proclaiming his hatred of money—and he has good reason to hate it. The lovers of money are willing to work for it. They know they are able to deserve it."[1]

There's nothing wrong with seeking financial success, and money isn't an evil to be cast out. It's easy to blame all that's wrong with the world on a little green piece of paper, but money is just an inanimate object. Objects themselves are neither good nor evil. It's the actions that people take and the ways in which people choose to let money negatively affect their lives that are the real problems.

Many people are good stewards of their money; they choose to use it in positive ways. There are also a lot of people who have huge money problems, but that's not the money's fault. Many people feel they've been wronged by money. They lay the blame for their money problems everywhere except where it really belongs: with themselves. If you're looking for the root of your money evils, look no further than the mirror.

Lots of people believe that their only problem with money is that they don't have enough of it. But this logic isn't sound. The actions you've chosen to take in your career, in your spending habits, in your investment accounts are what have led to your current financial situation. If you haven't managed a small amount of money well, there's no reason to believe you'd do better with a larger amount. If you're responsible with your money, no matter how much you start out with, it'll grow. If you're irresponsible with your money, no matter how much you start out with, it'll shrink. The money isn't the variable; the person in control of the money is.

It seems that capitalism is on the verge of becoming politically incorrect. Those who seek wealth are often seen as selfish and empty, lacking real moral values. We live in a society where mediocrity grows more and more acceptable, but your quest for increased wealth is an honorable one. Defend it with your words and actions. Don't let it become dishonorable by wanting more than you've earned, buying things you can't afford, or defaulting on your promises to pay.

There is, without question, much more to life than money. But I believe that the way you manage your finances says a lot about who you are. Let the way you manage your money be an opportunity for you to display your morals and principles. I want you to earn it, save it, invest it, and use it in a way that is reflective of your beliefs.

Using money for charity

I'm not a theologian, and this isn't a religion book. It's my hope that this book will provide sound financial advice for readers of all faiths. I can help you manage your money, but you have to manage your heart. I do think that a person's beliefs will play a significant role in her or his financial journey. Those beliefs will provide comfort in times of financial stress; they'll lead to gratitude in times of financial prosperity; and they'll affect financial decisions on issues such as giving.

I also think that donating to charity is good karma. According to Wikipedia, karma is the concept of "action" or "deed," understood as that which causes the entire cycle of cause and effect. When you put good out into the world, you will get good back, and when you put bad out into the world, you will get bad back. In other words, what goes around comes around.

Some of us donate to charity because it's part of our faith, and some of us do it because it's good karma. We also do it for a variety of other reasons, such as:

- \$ It makes us feel good.
- \$ It makes others feel good.
- \$ It enhances our own life when we enhance the lives of others.
- \$ We hope others would do it for us.
- \$ We want to make an impact.
- \$ We feel like it's our obligation.
- \$ We believe it's the right thing to do.

Charity begins at home

If you believe in charity, and hopefully you do, your quest can benefit not only you but others in need. The more you have, the more you have to share with others. However, I'm a firm believer in the idea that charity begins at home. Your first financial responsibility is to yourself and your family. If you're struggling to make ends meet, you really can't afford to give money away. Think back to the last time you were in an airplane. The flight attendant likely gave you instructions about a mask that would drop down from overhead if there was a change in cabin pressure. She or he probably demonstrated how to put it on, and then told you that if you were traveling with a child, you must secure your own mask before assisting the child. Charity is very similar. You have to get your own finances in order before you can help others in financial need.

For example, perhaps you would like to donate to a local college scholarship fund, but you have children of your own for whom you need to set the money aside. There's no shame in that. Remember: You have to put your own financial mask on before you can assist others. In addition, managing your own finances in a responsible way actually is a gift to the rest of society. It ensures that others will not have to foot the bill for your bad choices.

I find it very disheartening that many organizations soliciting donations will include a spot for you to supply your credit card information so you can charge your donation. Don't do it. If you have to put your donation on credit, you're in no position to be making it in the first place. Further, don't get talked into making monetary donations you can't afford for the status associated with them. Many organizations will publish your name as a member of a certain donor level, or give you other perks and recognition for donating. That's not what charity is really about.

Volunteer: give your time instead of your money

Am I suggesting that you should forget about helping others and only focus on yourself? Certainly not. What I'm suggesting is that giving doesn't have to mean writing a check, handing out cash, or buying things to donate. Time is also a valuable asset and one that can go a long way in making a positive impact.

Give yourself. Spend time doing work for your cause. People often worry when they give money about whether or not it's truly being put to good use. When you give your time, that worry no longer exists. You know exactly what kind of difference you're making. You get to see it firsthand.

Do the math

Here's an equation I hope will convince you that giving your time can be just as valuable as giving your money. Let's assume you want to donate $500 to one of your favorite charities. To determine how much your time is worth, calculate your hourly rate of pay. If you make $40,000 per year, your hourly rate of pay would be as follows:

$40,000 per year / 52 weeks per year / 40 hours per week = $19.23 per hour

Now divide the amount you want to donate by that hourly rate.

$500 / $19.23 per hour = 26 hours

If you spent just a little over two hours per month volunteering for your charity, it would be the equivalent of your $500 donation.

Volunteering can be financially beneficial for both you and the organization you're working with. Giving to others can put your own financial life into perspective by helping you find focus beyond material possessions and making you appreciate what you already have. In addition, volunteers are the lifeblood of many nonprofit organizations that are frequently scrambling for support. From the Red Cross to the local elementary school PTA, volunteers keep the wheels of progress turning. Without them, the organization couldn't accomplish its mission.

In every nonprofit organization I've ever worked with, there has come a time when the "we don't have enough volunteers" discussion has come up. And I've worked with enough of these organizations by now to know that it's almost always going to be true that 80 percent of the work is done by 20 percent of the people for a variety of different reasons.

You can only be generous on your own behalf. Don't count on everyone else around you to see it the same way. I've seen many get frustrated because they decided to organize an effort, such as making meals for a family in need, and then couldn't get enough people to sign up to help. Lack of volunteers is often a natural part of the volunteer environment, and that's okay. Unless you have the clout of Bono from U2, don't expect the entire world to rally for your cause. Your effort can be just as meaningful, even if it's small-scale. If you've volunteered with literacy programs or with disaster relief, or if you've held the door open for a woman with two kids and a bag of groceries in her arms, you've made a difference, and that's something money can't buy.

What makes a person want to volunteer? Nearly everyone these days has a schedule overflowing with activities and commitments, lots of places to go, and lots of things to do. Yet many make the time to volunteer for a cause they believe in.

I think, among other reasons, people volunteer because they want a positive experience. Seek out an organization that you feel good about donating your valuable time to. Remember: There's nothing wrong with wanting to be appreciated. Everyone needs positive feedback to know that their contributions are having an impact.

If you can afford to give monetary donations, do so. If not, give with your actions instead of your wallet. Give blood. Help with PTA activities. Spend some time at a nursing home. There are a hundred things you can do to make the world a better place that don't involve money. Helping others, while maintaining a healthy financial state at home, is a win-win situation for everyone.

Donating small dollars

As I walked into the grocery store recently to do my weekly grocery shopping, some students from the local high school handed me a slip of paper with a list of food items on it. They were collecting donations for the food pantry. This is the kind of charity that I like the most.

First of all, young people were involved, which I like for several reasons. Today's children are certainly among the most privileged in history, and I think it's excellent for them to see that not everyone is as fortunate. I also believe that involving children with charity today will ensure a spirit of giving continues into the future. Secondly, I like to donate locally. My children and I have volunteered at our local food pantry several times, and they have an excellent program. I enjoy giving to a place that I've been to and experienced. I realize there are people all around the globe that need help, but for me, local giving is the most rewarding. Third, I like to donate items. I prefer to donate things like food, clothing, and toys at Christmas, rather than give cash. So for me, this was the perfect charity opportunity.

When you're collecting for a cause or organization, you can always tell who's taken their turn handing out that slip of paper or sitting at that bake sale table, because they don't rush hurriedly past you without making eye contact. They stop. They make a donation, even if it's a small one, because they know how exciting it is to get any item for your collection or any amount of money in your jar when you're the one behind that table. They also know that every dollar collected can add up to a lot. They smile. They tell you good luck with your cause.

Maybe you're not yet in the position to make large donations. While you're working on getting your finances in order, be a small donor. Make a commitment to give just one or two dollars or items when an opportunity presents itself.

Donating larger dollars

According to statistics from Giving USA's Annual Report on Philanthropy for the Year 2011, charitable contributions by individuals, foundations, bequests, and corporations reached $298.42 billion in 2011. Of that $298.42 billion, individuals gave $217.79 billion.[2] I'm not going to tell you how much of your income I think you should donate to charity. I believe giving is a personal decision and one that you should make on your own. Just remember to make sure the amount you decide to give fits into your balanced budget.

With so many worthy causes, how do you narrow it down? We all want to see good things happen for children and animals. We all believe in education, a clean environment, and the arts. But when a cause truly speaks to you, it will ignite a passion within. You will no longer see your volunteer hours or contributed dollars as an obligation. You will give them happily and freely. You will look forward to the opportunity to give them, because your cause is an extension of who you are.

Frugal people will want to see their donations used in a frugal manner, but in a sea of worthy causes, how can you find a charity that is going to be the best possible

steward of your money? Givewell.org makes this statement on its Website: "We seek charities that are 'cost-
effective' in the sense of *changing lives as much as possible
for as little money as possible.*" Although they "do not assess
charities only—or primarily—based on their cost-effectiveness," I think it's still important to consider how much
a charity is spending on overhead and administrative costs
when making your choices.[3] It's common these days for
organizations to be in the news for paying their execu-
tives large salaries or for spending significant amounts of
money on things like buildings or office furniture.

If you're in agreement with the budgeting and administrative choices your organization makes, giving an unrestricted gift may work fine for you. Unrestricted gifts are
free from limitations and are put to use at the discretion
of the organization. When it comes to donations, however, I rarely give unrestricted gifts. I'm typically a restricted
gift donor, because I often don't agree with some of those
choices, but I still feel strongly enough about the organization itself that I would like to continue to donate. A restricted gift allows me to do just that. For example, rather
than give an unrestricted gift to my alma mater, I make a
gift that's restricted for use by the department of accounting. Several of the professors in that department were my
teachers when I was there. I credit them with providing
me with a solid accounting foundation and good professional career advice. In short, they helped me get where
I am today and, now that I have the ability to give back,

I'm certain that they will be good stewards of my money. Additionally, giving to a specific segment of the university makes me feel like my smaller donation can be used to make a larger impact, rather than just becoming another drop in the ocean. Giving a restricted gift means I get to designate which specific programs, projects, or activities I want my donation to support.

Another way to ensure your donation is making as large of an impact as possible is to give directly to those in need. I used to work with a man who would get the name of a needy family each year at Christmastime, and then buy food and presents for them and leave the donations on their porch. He couldn't take a tax deduction for this charitable contribution because he wasn't donating to a qualified organization, but that didn't matter. It was worth it to him, because he saw that every dollar he spent was going straight to the family. If this kind of giving appeals to you, local schools and churches can help you make sure your donation is going directly to those who need it.

If global giving is more your speed, consider thinking globally and acting locally. Many local organizations sponsor global causes. For example, your church might be collecting money to buy malaria nets for malaria-prone countries in Africa. By donating locally to global causes, you can feel more of a connection to the charity.

And if you want to be sure your charitable contribution is tax deductible, keep these points in mind:

$ Contributions must be made to a qualifying organization. You can't deduct donations to specific individuals or political organizations or candidates.

$ Contributions are deductible only if you itemize. They're not deductible if you take the standard deduction.

$ Pledges are not deductible. In order to deduct the contribution, you must have actually made the donation, not just a pledge.

$ Keep good, organized records in your tax file of how much you've contributed. For monetary donations, save a bank record or written confirmation from the organization. For property donations, get a written confirmation from the organization.

Sometimes being asked for a donation can create an awkward money moment. Perhaps you're in a rush and don't have time to pick up any extra food items. Perhaps you just donated to a similar cause last week. Or maybe you have a different cause you prefer to donate to. Many times we feel guilty for not contributing. We feel cheap or greedy for not being able to help every good cause. But remember this: Your charity is your business. You should spend your charitable dollars in the way you see most fit and not feel ashamed that you can't help everyone.

What should you do if you're asked to donate and, for whatever reason, you've decided not to make a contribution? A simple I'm not going to be able to donate, given in a friendly tone should do the trick. If the requestor continues to push, repeat yourself in a friendly tone and then end the conversation. Charity should be a feel-good moment for all parties involved. Don't let it become something associated with guilt or a strain on your wallet.

10

What You Should Teach Your Children

A lesson about children from a Disney princess

You know the story: Beautiful girl finds herself in trouble. Handsome prince saves girl. Girl and prince live happily ever after. It's the classic Disney formula. Cinderella, Snow White, Sleeping Beauty—all the greats have followed that same magic recipe.

So in 2009, when I took my daughters to see Disney's newly released animated blockbuster, *The Princess and the Frog*, I was prepared for more of the same. Needless to say, I was shocked when I realized that Disney had finally brought itself into the 21st century. Not only was Tiana the first African-American Disney princess, she also had career goals. She was working two jobs and saving her money so that someday she could buy her own restaurant. Along the way, she also discovered love with her prince, and realized that she needed to find a balance between work and play in order to be truly happy. At last, a fairy tale with some real-life, modern-day values. I don't know if all of those messages were obvious to the 10 and under set, but I left feeling inspired to wave my women's lib flag, letting everyone who asked me about the movie know that I thought it had some great things to teach the little princesses of today.

You can imagine my disappointment when I was watching TV a few days later and a commercial for the movie came on. It said something to the effect of "She's a girl with a dream to find her prince, but she's going to have to kiss a few frogs to get there." My first thought was, ain't that the truth; but my second thought was, wait a minute, that wasn't her dream. Her dream was to own a restaurant. But I guess at the end of the day, that doesn't sell as many movie tickets, or theme park tickets, or as much licensed merchandise.

Even though the TV spot glossed over the messages I had found so inspiring, I became determined to make my money message crystal clear. You have to teach your children how to manage money. We all want our children to find happiness, the kind that happens when you find true love and the kind that comes with being strong, independent, and self-sufficient. According to a national phone survey conducted for the American Institute of CPAs (AICPA) by Harris Interactive, 47 percent of parents expect to support their children until age 22 or older.[1] That's not a good statement on the future financial independence of our children.

According to the same survey, 30 percent of parents never talk to their kids about money or have only had one big talk with them, and, on average, kids are 10 years old when their parents have the first discussion with them about finances. When it comes to kids and money, an ounce of prevention is worth a pound of cure. It's never too early to start conversations with your children about money. As soon as your child has a concept of money, you should start having discussions with them about it. Talk to them about budgeting and responsible money management starting when they're young, and ramp up the frequency of those conversations throughout their high school years.

Whether it's with coins in a piggy bank or dollars in a bank account, you have to teach your children about money. Teach them how to spend it wisely, teach them to save at least 20 percent of it, and use an allowance and possibly their report card to teach them how to earn it.

Should your children know how much you have?

A frugal person's children will always think their parents have less than they really do. They'll look around and see other families living in bigger houses and driving fancier cars. Meanwhile they'll be living in the house that's a good investment and riding in an inexpensive car that looks decent and runs well. The fact that you're more interested in building your net worth, rather than racking up possessions and impressing others, may be something that's lost on your children right now. They may think it means that other families have more than you do but, as they get older, they'll understand that all along you were really just being smart with your money.

Of parents surveyed in one poll, 56 percent believe their high school graduates are totally unprepared to manage their personal finances responsibly.[2] Hello, parents. This means that 56 percent of you are not preparing your high school graduates for the task of managing their personal finances. Less than half of all states have a statewide financial education requirement, and only four states require a full semester course in personal finance.[3] That means the burden for this education falls on your shoulders and your shoulders alone. Children need lots of exposure to finances in order to master them. They won't get that exposure if you aren't willing to talk openly about money—not just theirs, but yours, too. Get them involved in your financial life. Ask for their help in creating your budget. Informing your children of your financial goals and priorities will help them be more understanding when the family has to make sacrifices or when you have to tell them no.

In addition to having regular financial discussions with your children, be ready to have money talks when opportunities present themselves. Significant times in a child's life offer good chances for you to talk about money. For example, back-to-school season is a great time for you to have a money talk. Back to school usually means more than just studying. It also means shopping. From clothes to shoes to book bags and supplies, for many kids back to school means a new wardrobe and a new backpack full of stuff. The first day of school is a prime time for children to examine how much they have in comparison to others, as they look around at everyone else's first day of school outfit.

So what should you do if your child comes to you asking for an expensive ensemble for the first day of school? There are two responses you can give. One, you can say, "Yes." But remember: You can only say yes if the item fits in your budget. And it's never too early to teach your children how to shop the sale racks or the clearance sections either. Two, you can use "I'd rather," and start establishing the difference between needs and wants. Say something like, "I know you want that outfit, but I don't think you need one that costs that much. I'd rather save that money for our summer vacation" or "I'd rather use that money for your soccer registration fees." There's nothing wrong with telling your children how you are and are not going to spend your money. You have to be willing to make those clear and direct money statements.

Children don't necessarily need to know specifically how much you make per year or have in your bank account balance. But they should know what your money priorities are. Whether your net worth is on track or whether you're still working on it, your children need to know that you're making conscious decisions with your money.

Plant the seed of frugality

As parents, it's a normal urge for us to want to give our children everything. We have the best of intentions. We want our kids to be happy, healthy, and successful. We want them to fit in.

Despite what you might expect, I'm not going to tell you that you shouldn't buy your children any fancy clothes or name-brand shoes for two reasons. First, it would make me a complete hypocrite. I have to admit I've dropped a pretty penny myself in the name of my children. Second, because you might be tempted to turn a deaf ear if I did. The urge to buy your little sweeties all of the treasures their hearts desire is a powerful one, so I'm not going to tell you to completely abstain.

Why wouldn't I do that? Wouldn't it go along with my frugal teachings? Maybe, but I think true frugality is something you have to grow into. It takes maturity, self-confidence, and a larger perspective on what's really important. Children are not at a place in their lives where they're able to completely embrace a frugal mentality. At this time in their lives, peer pressure is often high, and self-confidence and self-awareness are not yet fully developed.

Does this mean I think it's okay to shower them with lavish electronic gadgets and a closet full of designer clothes and shoes? No, of course not. But I do think there's a balance. If you exclude all name brands at this stage of the game, your children are likely to think of you as an old-fashioned drag. Every parent knows that the surest way to funnel your kid straight toward something is by putting a ban on it.

If you can give in to their requests in moderation, you'll be provided with some very good teachable moments, the first one being the importance of hard work and responsibility. I'm a firm believer in teaching your children about the results of both. If you're in a position to be able to buy nice things for your children, it's probably because you've put hard work and responsibility into practice in your own life. It's okay for your children to see that connection. In fact, it's okay for you to tell them that explicitly.

In addition, you need to teach them about the importance of character. If you buy them an expensive book bag, make sure you're also teaching them to appreciate the opportunity to attend school. If you buy them those pricey mechanical pencils, be certain you're also teaching them how valuable the skill of writing is. Also, make sure your children know that even if you buy them a North Face jacket or a hoodie from Abercrombie & Fitch, you believe that it's not the clothes that make the kid. Your children may be fortunate enough to have nice things, but see that they aren't forming their opinions of others on the basis of their belongings. Teach them that all of the cute outfits in the world don't add up to much in comparison to true friendship and laughter.

Teaching children about hard work, responsibility, and character is important, because in the adult world it will ultimately translate into financial success. Children who learn to appreciate what they have, who learn to value skills and a job well done, and not possessions, will be ready to let go of the name brands later in life and just hold on to those other lessons.

Allowances, budget money, and paying for grades

According to the AICPA survey, 61 percent of parents surveyed said they give their children an allowance. The average allowance is $65 per month.[4] The allowance you pay your children will depend on their age and the financial circumstances of your family. My suggestion when determining the amount you should pay is to err on the side of caution. It's hard to earn a buck out there in the real world. Uncle Sam's going to take part of it, and if you're lucky enough to have benefits, that'll eat up part of it, too. Before you know it, the amount you actually get to take home has dwindled. Don't set your children up for unrealistic expectations about how much they're going to get in their first paycheck by paying them an unusually large amount for the jobs they do at home.

The survey also showed that 88 percent of parents help pay for discretionary items for their children such as sports equipment, outings with friends, cell phones, movies, and media downloads. It seems that the allowance is an additional supplement to the money parents are already providing.

Create a line item within your budget for your children's expenses. Then, depending on their age, decide whether you want to administer their budget money or if you want to let them do it. For example, if you're going to give your child money for outings with their friends, set an amount and give it to them at the beginning of the month. When they want to go somewhere with their friends, let them know they will have to use that money. If it runs out before the end of the month, so be it. They'll have to look for free things to do. If they have extra, they can roll that money over to the next month. Older children can be put in charge of administering their own money for things such as clothes, school supplies, gas, and so on.

What if your child needed to buy soccer cleats with the money you gave them but instead bought a ticket to the midnight movie premiere, and a large popcorn and soda combo? Buy them the cleats and deduct the money you had to spend from the following month's allotment.

If you have younger children, the same concept can apply, but you'll have to do more of the administration of the money yourself rather than just turning it over to your child. For example, you might want to let your younger child administer their own "treat" budget. Set a certain amount that they can spend for the month on things like treats from the grocery store. This money can be used for a pack of gum, a bag of chips, or a cupcake from the bakery section. However, it may not be as easy for you to give them free reign over things like their clothing budget, unless you want their fall wardrobe to consist of three SpongeBob t-shirts and a pair of fuzzy slippers. Younger children will need more guidance in their money decisions, because they're not ready for the full course from the school of hard knocks just yet.

Children should be meeting normal expectations of contributing to the household in order to receive their budget money. They should be doing things like keeping their room and bathroom clean, keeping their things picked up around the house, and contributing to laundry and dishes as asked or needed. In addition, a pleasant attitude and good behavior should be normal household expectations. No nicey, no money. Period.

Am I advocating just handing money over to your children? If they're contributing to the household and if they're doing it with a smile (or at least not with a scowl), then I think it's reasonable that they receive some parental financial assistance; 88 percent of us are already doing that, anyway. What I want to focus on is the opportunity this provides to teach your children about budgeting and making money choices. Don't be an open checkbook. Set an amount, let them know what your expectations are (that is, this money is for school supplies), and then stick to it.

What about that traditional allowance? If you want to give money beyond your child's budget money, it should be for work above and beyond normal expectations, such as cleaning the car, cleaning out the garage, or baby-sitting younger siblings.

According to the AICPA survey, 48 percent of parents with children in school pay their children for good grades.

The average rate for an A is $16.60.[5] For kids, school is their job. That they attend school is a normal expectation, just like going to work every day is a normal expectation for adults. That they excel in school may very well be worth a financial reward.

I don't see anything wrong with paying for performance. It's commonplace in corporate America, and it can be effective when families apply it to schoolwork as well. If you decide to provide a monetary reward for grades, also emphasize work ethic to your children and teach them that money is not the only reason they should want to get good grades. They should also be doing it because it's the right thing to do.

Some parents feel philosophically opposed to paying for grades. If this doesn't match your values or beliefs, then don't do it. Some experts recommend rewarding behaviors such as good study habits or completing homework rather than the grade on the report card. This sounds good in theory, but doesn't always translate well in the real world. As my dad says, "Do you want a doctor that tries really hard or one that gets it right?"

Now, get ready for the most shocking AICPA survey statistic. Only 1 percent of parents say their children save any of their allowance.[6] One percent? It's no wonder our economy is in trouble when even our children are spending every penny as fast as they get it.

Whether it's budget money, allowance money, gift money, or whatever money it is, insist that your children save 20 percent of it. When it comes to children and money, saving is not a money choice; it's a money must. Teaching your children about budgeting is about teaching them how to make good money choices. Insisting that your children save is about creating a good habit. There are many things that we insist on with our kids. If your child never wanted to eat a vegetable at dinner, you wouldn't let him or her get away with it. When they're sick and undernourished, you wouldn't say, "They'll figure it out. It's their body, and they should be able to eat whatever they want." But we do that with money. We say, "It's their money. They should be able to do whatever they want with it, and when they're broke, they'll figure it out."

Your children can make their choices with 80 percent of their money, and you can let them make mistakes with that amount. It's okay for them to learn the hard way with that 80 percent. But again, insist that they save the other 20 percent. It's like allowing your child to have cereal for dinner but insisting that they eat at least three pieces of broccoli with it. And just like you make your children brush their teeth every night before bed, you have to make them save.

What about giving? Should you insist that they donate part of their money to charity? When it comes to charity, expose but do not impose. Charity comes from a different place. It comes from the heart, not out of habit. You can't just do it; you have to feel it. The chances for your children to become charitable are far better if you expose them to a variety of charitable opportunities. Get them involved in church fundraisers and outreach. Take them to a food pantry. Have them walk dogs at the local pound. By exposing your children to a variety of charities, you'll help them figure out what they're passionate about, and once they find their passion, you won't have to force them to donate. They'll want to do it.

One of the best things you can do when teaching your children about money is to put technology on your side. The lives of both kids and adults these days revolve around technology. As your kids get older, it's unlikely that they're going to be using only cash and even less so that they'll be using checks to pay for things. Debit cards and online payments will dominate their financial transactions.

When your child is old enough (I'd recommend 12 or older), help them set up a checking account with a debit card. This will typically require that you sign on the account as well if your child is under 18. Budget money or allowance money can be deposited into this account, and your child can get used to using plastic responsibly. Have them keep a small amount of cash on hand for situations where cards can't be used. Encourage them to check their banking online every day. If they have a smartphone, they can even log in and check their account through their phone. Also, remember to decline overdraft protection, so if your child tries to spend money that isn't available in the account the transaction will be declined.

Younger children may not be ready for a debit card. They'll be using cash, but you can still help them set up an account that comes with online banking. They can check it from time to time, rather than every day, to see how much they have. Help them make regular deposits so they can watch their account grow.

Keeping up with the Joneses, college style

A college education is a big-ticket item in a family budget. Do you feel an obligation to pay for your children's college education? College is a financial priority, just like retirement or purchasing a home. The first step in the process is assessing how much financial assistance you want to provide for your children. Do you want to pay for everything? Will you only pay for in-state schools? Are you willing to pay for two out of four years? If your children are old enough (middle school age and up), include them in the college discussions. Talk with them frankly about it, and let them know how expensive a college education can be.

If you want to finance your child's education, you'll have to make sacrifices. Sometimes you'll have to do without for the sake of your children. Sometimes you'll have to say no when they ask you to buy other things for them. On average, college tuition and fees increase by approximately 8 percent per year.[7] So if your child was just born, and the tuition and fees at the school you're looking at are currently $7,000 per year, you can expect them to be about $28,000 by the time your child is 18. Not only do you need to budget for tuition, fees, and room and board, you'll also need to budget for books, supplies, personal expenses, and transportation. Visit the Websites of some of your local colleges. They'll give you a full cost breakdown that you can use along with the 8 percent per year increase to estimate how much your child's education will cost.

When I say the words "college savings," most people think of the 529 Plan. Basically, you put dollars into a 529 account that can then be invested in a variety of ways. The money grows through time, and you use that money for your child's college education. Amounts deposited in the 529 account grow tax-free until distributed. Then the distributions are tax-free so long as they're not more than the beneficiary's adjusted qualified education expenses for the year.

However, saving for a college education doesn't have to only involve investment. There are some other basic things you can do to help finance your child's education. For example, forego your own education. That's a bold statement, but in many families, there's only so much money to go around. If your own continuing education isn't going to lead to a substantially better salary, you may want to think twice. We all have dreams, but every financial choice is a trade-off.

Another example would be to not wait until your child's senior year to start looking at scholarships. Know what the scholarship requirements are in advance so your child has plenty of time to put him or herself in the best possible position to receive an award. Lastly, take private and out-of-state schools off the table. Every state has at least one public, in-state school, and some larger states have more than 30. Take advantage of this.

Do the math

The average cost of a year of full-time tuition and fees in 2012–13[8] was as follows:

- \$ Community college: \$3,131.
- \$ Public in-state college: \$8,655.
- \$ Public out-of-state college: \$21,706.
- \$ Private college: \$29,056.

Your minimum cost for four years of college, two years at a community college and two years at a public in-state college, according to these averages would be (\$3,131 × 2) + (\$8,655 × 2), or \$23,572. This is a savings of \$11,048 over attending a public in-state college for four years, \$63,252 over attending a public out-of-state college for four years, and \$92,652 over attending a private college for four years.

Attending a public in-state college for four years will save you \$52,204 over attending a public out-of-state college for four years and \$81,604 over attending a private college for the same amount of time. Keep in mind that these figures don't include room and board. That will cost you, on average, an additional \$9,205 per year.

Students shouldn't put themselves in the position of having to take out large student loans. According to a report by the Institute for College Access and Success, two-thirds of college seniors graduated with loans in 2010 and carried an average debt of \$25,250. They also faced a high unemployment rate of 9.1 percent.[9]

Students need to seek out public in-state schools and also examine community college options. Many children want the college experience. This means picking the college of their dreams and living there, either in a dorm or in off-campus housing, for four years. Kids and parents need to reprioritize when it comes to college. The purpose of getting a college education is to get a better-paying job, so you can be in a better financial situation. If you're accumulating heavy debt to get that education, you're defeating the purpose.

Creating large amounts of student loan debt can start the next phase of a student's life off on the wrong foot. You might not enjoy the thought of your child attending community college or only considering public in-state schools. Maybe you can't imagine your child living at home while they attend school. These, however, are real, cost-saving options that you should seriously consider. Would you rather have your kids living with you while they're in college, or after they graduate, when they can't afford to support themselves because they've accumulated a mountain of debt?

Whenever I make the suggestion to take private schools off the table, I always get flak from people affiliated with private institutions who want to tell me about all the grants and scholarships they offer. Students at private colleges did receive an average total of $15,680 per year in grant aid and tax benefits for an average net cost of about $13,380 per year, but students at public institutions received an average $5,750 per year in grant aid and tax benefits, for an average net cost of just more than $2,900 per year.[10] Certainly there may be a situation where a particular scholarship available at a private college could completely cover tuition or bring it down to a level lower than the average, but this is true for public colleges as well. It's also important to note that about two-thirds of all full-time undergraduate students receive grant aid. But when colleges use the term "financial aid" and advertise a much higher percentage of students receiving this aid, that percentage includes those students who are receiving loans.

Every school has its advantages and disadvantages. College can be a wonderful experience for your child, but just how much are you willing to pay for that experience? Like everything else in life, there's a limit. We like to believe that all options are open to us when in reality we are, or should be, bound by financial restraints. The good news is that students will get out of their education what they put into it in time and effort, not money. That's why I'm such an advocate of choosing a low-cost option. The beginning of college marks the beginning of a new adventure. With some proper planning, it can be a time of excitement rather than financial stress.

Set a good example

Setting a good example for your children is one of the most important things you'll ever do with your money. It's necessary to be a good financial role model in order to ensure that your children have a bright financial future. The children of today are smarter and savvier than ever.

They won't fall for the "do as I say, not as I do" kind of parenting. For the sake of your children, don't be a financial hypocrite.

If you ask them to budget their money, make sure you're budgeting yours. If you tell them to save 20 percent of their money, make sure you're saving 20 percent of yours. If you can't afford to do that right now, tell them that. Don't expect them to be mind readers, and don't expect them to do things that are the complete opposite of what they see you doing. Let them know that you're getting your finances in order and keeping them in order. While you're working on finding and nurturing your frugal side, help your children nurture theirs. If you plant the seeds early on, as they get older, you'll be able to watch their frugality grow.

11

Achieving Financial Success

The simple formula

No one can predict the future—not your financial advisor, not the local palm reader, not even your CPA. If I had a guaranteed get-rich equation, I wouldn't be sitting here at my computer typing this book. I'd be lying on a beach in Hawaii perfecting my tan and sipping one of those drinks with an umbrella in it.

I can't tell you when the stock market is going to recover. I can't tell you when the housing market is going to recover. I can't even tell you when the Real Housewives are going to recover from their latest round of plastic surgery. And anyone who says they can is, to put it frankly, full of it. But there is a formula I've found to be true nearly all of the time, and I'm willing to let you in on it for free:

Hard work + responsible spending = financial success.

Your income and expenses are the two things you have control over. You can't control the stock market or the housing market, and right now you may feel like you can't control the labor market. But even with unemployment on the economic forefront this is still America, the land of opportunity, and opportunity exists around every corner for those who are willing to work hard for it.

There are many people out there who would like to tell you how to get rich by doing things like selling their products, buying foreclosed homes, or starting Internet-based businesses. I'm not against those things. They can all be profitable ventures, but despite what you may be led to believe, they all take much time and effort. In fact, so does almost anything that's going to earn you a substantial income. Unless you're one of those lucky lottery winners, you're going to have to work hard for your money. Don't expect something for nothing. Stop looking for a way to make a lot by doing just a little. The reality is that most of the time, life doesn't work that way.

The second part of the formula, responsible spending, is just that simple. For some reason, the human race loves to over-complicate things. We discuss, we analyze, and we discuss some more. But let me make it elementary. If you want to experience greater financial success, stop spending so much darn money. You don't need me to tell you that; it's common sense. Knowing it is the easy part. It's applying it in everyday life that's difficult. It's much easier to search for the get-rich-quick answer than focusing on spending less, because spending responsibly is often hard work, too. It requires budgeting, choosing, and engaging your frugal mind. So that is my secret formula. It isn't glamorous or flashy. It wouldn't make for a very good infomercial, but it will put you well on your way to a successful financial future.

Commit to the mental shift

What else must you do in order to be on your way to a successful financial future? You need to commit to making the mental shift. If you only go through the motions of creating a balanced budget, which includes decreased spending and increased savings, but don't commit to the mental shift, it won't last. You won't be able to follow through with sticking to your budget. A budget can't be a dead document that you begrudgingly open up and refer to every once in a while. It has to be alive in your mind and in your actions each and every day when you make big and little financial choices. Putting a budget in writing without frugality in mind is about as useful as lipstick on a pig, but if you change your mindset, you'll also change your money.

Incorporate a frugal mentality into all of your financial decisions. Think frugally every time you choose to spend, and ask yourself if it would be wiser to save instead. Think frugally when you make large purchases, such as a home and a car. Model frugality for your children.

When you commit to the mental shift, you commit to a life in which you're happier and richer, both with money and beyond money. Start now, and I mean right now. Don't wait until the first of the month or the 15th of the month. Don't wait until Sunday or Monday or until after your birthday or Christmas has passed. Don't wait another minute. Make frugal thinking a part of your daily life, starting now.

Incorporate change into your daily life

The Merriam-Webster Dictionary lists one definition of change as, "to replace with another." Start replacing your old money habits with new ones and your bad money habits with good ones. Then, don't slip back into old habits. Once you've decided to make a change, keep moving forward, even if it's only a little at a time. You can do that by keeping your priorities straight. Put them in writing. Refer to them and keep them at the forefront of your mind when making money choices. Eliminate things that are counterproductive to your priorities, and stay away from places that tempt you to overspend.

Set yourself up for success by using the tools around you to make change as easy and painless as possible. Utilize technology such as spreadsheet programs, online banking, and smartphone applications to make budgeting, sticking to your budget, and paying your bills easier. The world of technology can seem complicated, but in reality, technology can help make your finances simpler, and you know I'm all about keepin' it simple.

We're a society of instant gratification. We like to see immediate results. Right now you probably feel a strong sense of urgency to get your finances in order, and that's great. That sense of urgency will kick-start your frugal mind and motivate you to start down a better financial road. Accomplishing short-term goals is vital. It keeps our battery charged and our spirits up. Achieve as many short-terms goals as you can as quickly as you can. If you follow the advice in this book, you'll see immediate results, but to reach your full financial potential, you need to be in it for the long-run, internalizing a frugal mentality and continuing to educate yourself financially. Therefore, long-term goals are just as important, and when it comes to your long-term financial outlook, remember: Slow and steady wins the race.

Real change takes time. There are things you can do right away to start improving your finances. Putting together a balanced budget is a relatively quick exercise. It should only take a few hours to get your budget down in writing. However, monitoring your budget by checking your online banking daily is a habit that takes more time to become engrained. Learning how to stick to your budget is also something that will take more time.

You can immediately start chipping away at your debt but, depending on how much debt you've racked up, it might take a while to completely dig yourself out. Again, the important thing is to stick with it. You can also start increasing your savings right away. Even if your account doesn't immediately grow by leaps and bounds, if it's growing, that's better than shrinking. Take each small step as a success and build on those successes.

I'm not asking you to do anything you can't handle. Making a change is like riding a roller coaster; there will be ups and downs. Some days will be more fun than others. Some days you'll stick to your budget, and pride in yourself will swell. Other days you'll have to pass something up because it's not in your budget, and you won't feel so great. But make the change and you'll see that making responsible decisions with your money doesn't limit you; it actually opens up a whole new world of possibilities.

Put it all together

People tend to think of finance as some kind of abstract or intangible concept. Hopefully, through the stories I've shared with you, I've been able to show you that real financial lessons are all around us in our daily lives. You may not have noticed them or been paying attention to them, but they are there. They're there to remind us that anyone can become an expert in the subject matter of their own finances if they're willing to take these lessons and apply them to their money choices. Don't let yourself or anyone else try to make it too complicated. Just follow the steps I've laid out in this book and start putting one foot in front of the other.

Here are some important things you can do:

$ Find your frugal side and create a financial support group that will nurture your frugal mentality. This group will share your goals and help you work toward them. They'll challenge and support you on your financial journey. Hopefully, this group will include your friends and family members. Let them know what your financial goals are. Money is not a dirty word and your financial goals don't have to be top-secret information. When you do things in isolation, you're less likely to succeed. When your goals are out in the open, it's easier for others to encourage you. If no one knows what you're aiming for, they won't know how to support you on your journey. To be successful, it's important to utilize the support of others.

$ Create a balanced budget that includes paying off your debt. As of the end of June 2012, 46.7 percent of American households carried a credit card balance and the average balance was $15,597.[1] Creating a balanced budget ensures you will not dig yourself into that hole again.

$ Save more than the average. As of the end of June 2012, the personal savings rate was 4.3 percent.[2] Who wants to be average? You can do better than that.

$ Make it a goal to educate yourself about your investment options. Education will make a huge difference in your financial future.

$ Be sure you're making good decisions when you make large purchases. Large purchases can have a big impact on your finances.

$ Focus on net worth. Increase your assets; decrease your liabilities.

$ Give, in whatever way you are able.

$ Involve your children in the process. Start teaching them about money today, so they can be successful with it tomorrow.

$ Work to increase your income with your long-term financial future in mind, even though it may not happen overnight. If you're unemployed, fill out those applications. If you're working, go above and beyond each day to stand out to your employer and your customers. If you do your job well, whether working for yourself and building your business, or working for someone else and climbing the ladder, taking control of your income will mean taking control of your financial destiny.

$ Stay positive and measure your progress. The right attitude can really help you and the wrong attitude can really hinder you. Getting down on yourself isn't going to get you anywhere, but neither is kidding yourself. Be realistic and honest. Give yourself small rewards as you reach milestones on your financial journey. For example, when you create a budget and stick to it for six months, or when your emergency fund has six months' worth of living expenses, reward yourself. Remember: These rewards don't have to cost much money. Think pat on the back rather than lavish party. Also, expect a few setbacks. When you do have one, analyze what went wrong and why, and get right back on that horse.

Live better

Wikipedia refers to change as "the process of becoming different," but I don't want you to just live differently. I want you to live better. Living better doesn't mean having more stuff. It means breaking the chains of debt and overspending, so you can experience the freedom and peace of mind that good money management will bring. It means creating a bright future for you and your children. And you can do it. Living beyond your means is a choice, but a bad one. You can't be free mentally or financially if you have large amounts of debt hanging over your head. But you can start making better choices each and every day.

Living within your means doesn't mean living a life of abstinence. It means living a life where you can be proud of the choices you make. It means exploring ideas and activities that are both low-cost and fun. You can feel responsible, smart, and confident, because you've mastered your money. You can live better, because you'll be spending quality time with the people that mean the most to you.

We live in a world that's become increasingly materialistic. People are much more concerned about being fashion savvy than they are about being financially savvy. Living better doesn't mean choosing between one or the other. It means doing both. I want you to buy a knock-out outfit on clearance and put the leftover money right into a savings or investment account. Full price is foolish. You don't have to be frumpy, but nothing wears better than smart.

It falls on the shoulders of us Gen Xers and Gen Yers to stop the debt train our country is on. We have to say enough with the ridiculous credit card loans, home equity loans, car loans, and student loans. We have to become a generation that buys things, goods and services, which we can afford. We have to become good role models for our children. If we don't, the burden will fall to them, and they'll be ill-equipped to handle it. We want them to be able to live better, too. It's time to break the financial taboo. Start talking to people about money; talk to your kids, your family, and your friends. Discuss it more often than you discuss what happened on the latest episode of Honey Boo Boo.

Nobody's perfect. In the introduction to this book, I told you how I overdrew my checking account and CPAs everywhere rolled over in their grave as I admitted to less than flawless execution in my own financial life. Would you admire me more if I told you that I'd never had a financial mishap, never squandered a penny or forgotten to pay a bill? I don't think so. I've never been a financial advisor to the stars, and I've never gone through the huge ups and downs of amassing a fortune and losing it. What I have been is a turtle. I'm a regular girl, who's lived a regular life and worked a regular job in a regular little town. And slowly and steadily, I'm winning the race. If I can do it, you can do it.

It's easy to be tempted. There will always be times when a bigger house, a newer car, an expensive pair of shoes start calling our name. For a moment we think, "I want that. I want to live there. I want to drive that. I want to wear that." It's okay to have those thoughts, but you can't let them take over and influence your financial decisions. In order to defeat that temptation, stay grounded in what's really important—that is, the things money can't buy: relationships and connections with friends and family, quality time with them, and memories that are made. None of these are dependent on the size of your house, model of your car, or brand of your shoes. Remind yourself of that every time temptation comes knocking at your door.

I know you can cut through the clutter of today's constant commercialism. You don't really believe that the stuff you own is the most important thing in your life. You're smarter than that. You know the value of the things money can't buy. You're ready to get out of the trap of overspending and do what needs to be done to get your finances in order. I know there's a frugal person inside you just waiting to be released. I know you can spend less, save more, and live better.

Notes

Chapter 1

1. "Head Over Heels: ShopSmart Poll Finds Women Own 17 Pairs of Shoes," PRNewswire.com, *www. prnewswire.com/news-releases/head-over-heels-shopsmart-poll-finds-women-own-17-pairs-of-shoes-117967459.html.*

Chapter 2

1. "360 Degrees of Financial Literacy, Financial Literacy: Knowing What You Need to Know to Achieve Your Financial Goals," AICPA.org, *www. aicpa.org/volunteer/financialliteracyresourcecenter/*

volunteermobilizationkits/generalfinancialliteracy/ downloadabledocuments/financial_literacy_speech_final_10-4.pdf.

2. John Cothren and JoAnne Gryder, "Drought Affecting Corn Production; Expect Higher Prices in Many Food Staples and Products," NC State University: NC A&T State University Cooperative Extension Wilkes County Center, July 18, 2012.

3. Official USDA Food Plans: Cost of Food at Home at Four Levels, U.S. Average, June 2012, CNPP. USDA.gov, *www.cnpp.usda.gov/Publications/Food-Plans/2012/CostofFoodJun2012.pdf.*

4. Dr. Seuss, *How the Grinch Stole Christmas!* (New York: Random House, 1957).

Chapter 4

1. "GDP Growth Slows in Second Quarter," U.S. Department of Commerce Bureau of Economic Analysis, September 27, 2012, BEA.gov, *www. bea.gov/newsreleases/national/gdp/2012/pdf/ gdp2q12_3rd_fax.pdf.*

Chapter 5

1. "The 2012 Consumer Financial Literacy Survey," Harris Interactive Inc. Public Relations Research, prepared for the National Foundation for Credit

Counseling and The Network Branded Prepaid Card Association (2012), NFCC.org, *www.nfcc.org/newsroom/FinancialLiteracy/files2012/FLS-2012FINALREPORT0402late.pdf.*

Chapter 6

1. "Depreciation Infographic: How Fast Does My New Car Lose Value?" September 24, 2010, Edmunds.com, *www.edmunds.com/car-buying/how-fast-does-my-new-car-lose-value-infographic.html.*

Chapter 7

1. "Debt," Thomas Jefferson Encyclopedia (February 9, 2011), Monticello.org, *www.monticello.org/site/research-and-collections/debt.*

2. Gaye Wilson, "Monticello Was Among the Prizes in a Lottery for a Ruined Jefferson's Relief," *Colonial Williamsburg Journal*: Winter 2010.

3. "MC Hammer Biography," LyricsFreak.com, *www.lyricsfreak.com/m/mc+hammer/biography.html.*

4. "10 Famous Cases of Celebrity Bankruptcy," The List Blog—Top 10, September 3, 2009, Listzblog.com, *www.listzblog.com/top_ten_cases_of_celebrity_bankruptcy.html.*

5. Jeff Reeves, "10 Most Embarrassing Celebrity Bankruptcies of All Time," February 14,

2012, InvestorPlace.com, *http://investorplace.com/2012/02/10-most-embarrassing-celebrity-bankruptcies-of-all-time/*.

6. "Monticello, Virginia," National Park Service, NPS.gov, *www.nps.gov/nr/travel/presidents/jefferson_monticello.html*.

7. "Net Worth: How do you stack up?" CNNMoney/CNN.com, *http://cgi.money.cnn.com/tools/networth_ageincome/*.

Chapter 8

1. Dennis Jacobe, "Work Is Labor of Love for Small-Business Owners," Gallup.com, August 23, 2005, *www.gallup.com/poll/18088/work-labor-love-smallbusiness-owners.aspx*.

2. "Get Ready," U.S. Small Business Administration, SBA.gov, *www.sba.gov/sites/default/files/files/sbfaq.pdf*.

3. "Number of Jobs, Labor Market Experience, and Earnings Growth: Results from a National Longitudinal Survey News Release," U.S. Department of Labor Bureau of Labor Statistics National Longitudinal Survey of Youth 1979, 2010–11, published July 25, 2012 by the U.S. Bureau of Labor Statistics.

4. Thinkexist.com, accessed April 2013, *http://thinkexist.com/quotation/the_key_to_everything_is_patience-you_get_the/222137.html.*

5. "Trends in College Pricing 2012," College Board Advocacy and Policy Center, Trends.collegeboard.org, *http://trends.collegeboard.org/sites/default/files/college-pricing-2012-full-report_0.pdf.*

6. Hannah Shaw and Chad Stone, "Key Things to Know About Unemployment Insurance," Center on Budget and Policy Priorities, CBPP.org, *www.cbpp.org/cms/?fa=view&id=3646.*

7. "The Employment Situation—February 2013," United States Department of Labor, Bureau of Labor Statistics (March 8, 2013), BLS.gov, *www.bls.gov/news.release/empsit.nr0.htm.*

Chapter 9

1. Ayn Rand, *Atlas Shrugged* (New York: Random House, 1957).

2. "Giving USA 2012—The Annual Report on Philanthropy for the Year 2011, 57th Annual Issue," researched and written at The Center on Philanthropy at Indiana University, published by Giving USA, *Alysterling.com, www.alysterling.com/documents/GUSA2012ExecutiveSummary.pdf.*

3. "Guide to Cost-Effectiveness Analysis," Givewell. org, *www.givewell.org/international/technical/criteria/cost-effectiveness.*

Chapter 10

1. "AICPA Survey Reveals What Parents Pay Kids for Allowance, Grades," Harris Interactive Inc. Public Relations Research (prepared for the American Institute of Certified Public Accountants), AICPA. org, *www.aicpa.org/Press/PressReleases/2012/Pages/ AICPA-Survey-Reveals-What-Parents-Pay-Kids-for-Allowance-Grades.aspx.*

2. Lewis Mandell, "The Jump$tart Survey," Jumpstart.org, *www.jumpstart.org/assets/ files/2008SurveyBook.pdf.*

3. "State Financial Education Requirements," Jump start.org, *http://jumpstart.org/state-financial-education-requirements.html.*

4. "AICPA Survey Reveals What Parents Pay Kids for Allowance, Grades," Harris Interactive Inc. Public Relations Research (prepared for the American Institute of Certified Public Accountants), AICPA. org, *www.aicpa.org/Press/PressReleases/2012/Pages/ AICPA-Survey-Reveals-What-Parents-Pay-Kids-for-Allowance-Grades.aspx.*

5. Ibid.

6. Ibid.

7. "Tuition Inflation," Finaid.org, *www.finaid.org/savings/tuition-inflation.phtml.*

8. "Trends in College Pricing 2012," College Board Advocacy and Policy Center, Advocacy.collegeboard.org, *http://advocacy.collegeboard.org/sites/default/files/college-pricing-2012-full-report_0.pdf.*

9. "Student Debt and the Class of 2010," The Project on Student Debt, An Initiative of the Institute for College Access and Success, Projectonstudentdebt.org, *http://projectonstudentdebt.org/files/pub/classof2011.pdf.*

10. "Trends in College Pricing 2012," College Board Advocacy and Policy Center, Advocacy.collegeboard.org, *http://advocacy.collegeboard.org/sites/default/files/college-pricing-2012-full-report_0.pdf.*

Chapter 11

1. "American Household Credit Card Debt Statistics through 2012," Nerdwallet.com, *www.nerdwallet.com/blog/credit-card-data/average-credit-card-debt-household/.*

2. "Comparison of Personal Saving in the National Income and Product Accounts (NIPAs) with Personal Saving in the Flow of Funds Accounts (FFAs)," U.S. Department of Commerce Bureau of Economic Analysis, BEA.gov, *www.bea.gov/national/nipaweb/Nipa-Frb.asp.*

Index

Allowances, 194-197

Ambition, 170

American Institute of
 CPAs (AICPA), 188,
 194, 196, 197

Assets, 139-150

Association of Independent
Consumer Credit Counseling
 Agencies, 82

Atlas Shrugged, 172

ATM withdrawals, 61

Back-to-school season, 191

Balanced budget, 47-48

Banking, online, 60-63, 197

Bankruptcy, 46

Bargain Brand Challenge,
 35-36, 52

Biofuels, 51

Black Friday, 69

Bonuses, 95

Braxton, Toni, 138

Brokerage firms, 103-104,
 112-113

Budget, trimming your,
 49-60

Budget, your children and,
 194-197

Budgeting, 43-71

Budgets, holidays and, 66-68

Bulk, buying in, 52

Bureau of Labor Statistics, 158

Busey, Gary, 138

Cable TV, 50

CDs, 106

Character, 193

Charity, 174-176, 179-185, 198-199

Checking account, children and, 199-200

Children, finances and your, 187-205

Children, saving and, 197-198

Christmas, 68-71

Clemens, Samuel, 137

College, paying for, 200-204

Contract work, 165

Corporate America, 167-170

Coupons, 53

Credit Card Accountability Responsibility and Disclosure Act, 60-61, 62

Credit cards, 18-19, 38-40, 46, 76, 77-79, 213

Credit cards, multiple, 78-79

Credit counseling, 82

Credit repair, 80-82

Credit report, 80-82

Debit cards, 38-40, 46, 199-200

Debit cards, children and, 199-200

Debt counselors, 82

Debt, 18, 73-82, 88

Differentiation, 120-122

Discipline, finances and, 46

Disney, 187-188

Donating money, 179-185

Eating out, 56-57

Education, 159

Einstein, Albert, 89

Embarrassment, finances and, 46

Employee Stock Purchase Plans, 110-113

Entertainment, 57

Entrepreneur, unrealistic, 156-157

Equifax, 80, 81

Eternal student, 159-160

Example, setting a good, 204-205

Excel, 47

Experian, 80, 81

Extreme couponing, 53-55

Failure, small business, 157

Fair Credit Reporting Act, 80

Federal Trade
    Commission, 80

Finances, discipline and, 46

Finances, embarrassment
    and, 46

Finances, your children
    and, 187-205

Financial education, 18-19

Financial literacy, 102-103

Financial success, 167-175

Financial support group,
    212-213

529 Plans, 201

Flipping houses, 114

401(k), 103, 107, 109

Generic brands, 52

Gifts, 96-97

Givewell.org, 182

Giving USA, 181

Glasgow, Arnold H., 158

Groceries, 50-56

Grocery store discount
    card, 51

Guilt, 44

Hammer, MC, 136-137, 139

Harmenszoon can Rijn,
    Rembrandt, 137

Holidays, budgets and,
    66-68

Home, buying a, 117-125

Houses, flipping, 114

*How the Grinch Stole
    Christmas!,* 70

Income, 151-166

Income, spouse's, 163-164

Inheritance, 96

Instant gratification, 211

Institute for College
    Access and Success, 202

Investing, 99-116

IRA, 103, 107, 109-110

Jefferson, Martha Wayles, 134

Jefferson, Thomas, 131-136

Job hopper, 158-159

Job, second, 165

Karma, 175

Kessinger, Saxon N. White, 170

KISS Principle, 27

Knight, Suge, 138

Large purchases, 117-129

Lechter, Sharon, 19

Leftovers, 52
Liabilities, 139-150
Literacy, financial, 102-103
Mental shift, 209-210
Menu planning, 52
Microsoft Excel, 47
Miracle cure, 26
Moderation, 59
Money, 167-175
Money, your children and, 187-205
Mortgage, 123-125
National Foundation for Credit Counseling, 82, 103
Negotiation, 128-129
Net worth, 131-150, 190, 214
Networking, 162-163
New Year's resolutions, 40
Nichols, Wilson Cary, 134
Oil prices, 51
Online banking, 60-63, 197
Overdraft protection, 61
Paying for college, 200-204
Paying for grades, 194-197
Paying off debt, 73-76
Personal savings, 87, 213
Phone service, 50

Positivity, 30
Post, Bud, 136-137
Princess and the Frog, The, 187-188
Purchases, large, 117-129
Quaid, Randy, 138
Rand, Ayn, 172
Real estate, 114-116, 117-120
Realization, 26
Responsible spending, 208-209
Restaurants, 56-57
Retirement, 93-94, 110
Roth IRA, 110
Satellite TV, 50
Saving, 83-97, 213
Saving, children and, 197-198
Savings plan, 87-95
Second job, 165
Services, trading, 165
Shift, mental, 209-210
Shopping list, 51-52
Shopping, 58
Small business failure, 157
Social media, 163
Spending, responsible, 208-209

Spouse's income, 163-164

Student loans, 18, 76, 203

Student, eternal, 159-160

Support group, 212-213

Take-home pay, 47-48

Tax refunds, 95-96

Time, volunteering, 177-179

Trading services, 165

Traditional IRA, 110

TransUnion, 80, 81

Trimming your budget, 49-60

Twain, Mark, 137

Tyson, Mike, 138

U.S. Small Business Administration, 157

Unemployed, 160-161

Unrealistic entrepreneur, 156-157

USDA, 55

Vacations, 127-128

Vehicle, buying a, 126-127

Volunteering, 177-179

Work, contract, 165

About the Author

Clare K. Levison is a certified public accountant and national financial literacy spokesperson for the American Institute of Certified Public Accountants (AICPA). She has appeared on major radio and television networks across the country and has served as a member of the Virginia Society of Certified Public Accountants (VSCPA) Board of Directors. She was named one of the 2010 Top Five CPAs Under Thirty-Five by the VSCPA. Clare has more than a decade of corporate accounting experience and is also an active volunteer, serving as PTA president, Girl Scout leader, and Sunday school teacher. She lives in Blacksburg, Virginia, with her husband and two daughters.